THE SECRET TECHNIQU

SEBASTIAN MARTIN SELBY

A SIMPLE MODERN APPROACH TO POP AND RAP
VOCAL MASTERY IN *16* THRILLING SINGING LESSONS

DESIGNED FOR KIDS, ADULTS,
SINGING TEACHERS & VOICE COACHES

INCLUDING THE MONUMENTAL ESSAY

The Art of Singing without Singing

Published by Songetry

Copyright © Sebastian Martin Selby, 2020

All rights reserved.
No part of this publication may be reproduced, distributed, or transmitted in any form or by any means, including photocopying, recording, or other electronic or mechanical methods, without the prior written permission of the publisher, except in the case of brief quotations embodied in critical reviews and certain other non commercial uses permitted by copyright law. For further questions, enquiries, information or permission requests, email songetry@ymail.com

ISBN: 9798692025388

Cover photography by bantersnaps
Front and back cover design by Priscilla Louzai

Let your light so shine before men, that they may see your good works and glorify your Father in heaven.

The Secret Technique Revealed is dedicated to my ever remarkable and enigmatic mother

This book is also dedicated to my great friend and mentor
Bruce (Ashare) Ruffin

Special thanks to Priscilla Louzai and David Lewis
for their invaluable support, guidance and direction
as this book neared release

Sometimes in life you have to just stand up and be fearless.
Don't think too much about the consequences, because the consequences may never come to pass. Do what you have to do before there is no time left do it. Brave the possible unkind glare or spoken word, because the thing that you are doing is greater than your fear of what it might ignite. It is your duty to let it be heard, seen and known, and it is your duty to be true to who you are,
and the life you have been given.

The Secret Technique Revealed manual
is an example of what I describe as writing to
awake, inform, inspire and incite.

Bring out the *light* within you–your unique vocal tone. Not everyone will possess an outstanding singing voice, but everyone *will* have their own unique tone. My book, The Secret Technique Revealed, will teach you how to bring out that unique tone, and make that unique tone shine — **Sebastian Martin Selby**

Songetry logo designed by Sebastian Martin Selby and Monica Campbell Artwork by Amara Norman. Songetry Lettering produced by Martin Weiland

CONTENTS

Introduction 1

Lesson 1   A Solid Singing Foundation 6

Lesson 2   Starting From In The Middle 26

Lesson 3   Singing With Your Mind 32

Lesson 4   Slow The Whole Thing Down 37

Lesson 5   Singing Out 40

Lesson 6   Making The Notes Come From Your Stomach 42

Lesson 7   Throat Disengagement 47

Lesson 8   Heading For The Sky And Digging Deep 51

Lesson 9   The Impact Voice 58

Lesson 10   It's All In The Phrasing 61

Lesson 11   The Seeking Mind Frame 67

Lesson 12   Counting On The Divine 69

Lesson 13   The Vocal Stronghold 73

Lesson 14   A Question Of Vocal Identity 76

Lesson 15   Capturing The Magic 79

Lesson 16   Revolution In The Mist 86

Essay   The Art Of Singing Without Singing 91

Afterword 145

Glossary 146

INTRODUCTION ...
The voice is unique among musical instruments ... You don't need your hands or feet to play it

Hi there! My name is Sebastian Martin Selby, and I am an expert in the field of pop vocal training and education. I am also a pop historian, as well as an essayist, novelist, poet and tunesmith. Concerning pop vocal training and education, I like to refer to myself as a vocal adviser, and I will be offering you top-notch advice on learning how to sing from this moment forth.

The Secret Technique Revealed, caters to all levels of vocal ability, from the complete beginner to the seasoned professional. If you are a rapper, you can also enjoy the information I will be sharing. Vocal coaches can use this manual alongside their usual teaching methods. Schools, colleges, and universities can use or incorporate this manual as or part of a pop vocal training programme of study on their music syllabus.

For those who have an interest or desire to explore their voice more seriously, this instruction manual is an excellent starting point. The lessons will help you quickly realise the potential of your voice; giving you a shorter route towards a professional vocal sound. If you approach my teaching with an open mind, you can change your vocal life for the better.

I set out to make this manual the only thing you will ever need regarding learning how to sing; a go-to lifelong companion containing all the answers, with everything you need to know at your fingertips; a manual capable of pointing you in the right direction, every time. I have left no stone unturned in my quest to make the acquisition and art of popular singing accessible to all and sundry, and therefore I put every drop of my vocal training knowledge on these pages.

THE SECRET TECHNIQUE REVEALED

No matter what genre of popular music you sing, this manual will be an invaluable resource for furthering your vocal ambitions. The lessons are suitable for children and adults alike. Most of the key concepts are simple enough for a child to grasp; so if you are the parent of a keen or talented child singer, this manual will prove invaluable for aiding your child's vocal development.

We all need help, advice or guidance at various stages in our vocal lives. The craft of singing is an ever-evolving one, even more so when you are just starting out. My writing aims to eliminate much of the bewilderment that begets newbie singers regarding vocal improvement. If you want to take your voice to the next better-sounding level, then going about things in the right way is all-important. Doing things the wrong way will only set back your voice and delay your goals.

When you are first learning how to sing your voice is a mystery to you. Slowly the mystery unravels as you get to know and understand your voice more and more. Learning how to sing equals getting to know and understand your voice (meaning to realise your voice's technical capabilities and limits.) The vocal adviser needs to get to know and understand your voice also if they are to guide you correctly. This manual offers you a Solid Singing Foundation and will give you all the guidance you need, as you build your vocal technique from the ground up.

The most important thing concerning the use of this manual is that you can sing in tune, and this manual goes on the premise you have no issues regarding correct pitching.

You will encounter many original terms along the way as you read through my work. I created these terms to make learning how to sing as elementary as possible. I also wanted to create a wholly new vocal vernacular for the modern-day vocal coach or singing teacher to have at their disposal when coaching or teaching their students.

You will not find any scale-based singing exercises included in this manual, which is in stark contrast to most written media that offer to teach you how to sing. My teaching is more geared towards vocal technique and singing mindset than anything else.

INTRODUCTION

Singing along with scales will prove beneficial to your voice in many respects: pitching, tuning, intonation, voice strengthening and range extension. Scale implementation is a voice investment and is something I encourage you to explore alongside using this manual. The Web will prove to be an excellent resource for aiding you. So make a point of introducing scales into your home-based practice sessions, sooner rather than later.

On the whole, I champion the one-to-one, hands-on approach. Training by singing example, and inspiring vocal improvement and awareness through spot-on instruction and advice, honest critical analysis and thought-provoking discussion. And it's in this respect that I see myself as a vocal adviser rather than say a vocal coach or singing teacher, who invariably base their teaching around the piano keys. A vocal adviser's chief concern is the making of the singer; the adviser's advice should have an accumulative effect that stirs the singer towards achieving vocal greatness.

I love to put things as fuss-free and straightforward as I can, without throwing lots of anatomy-based explanations at you. You can readily look into such things yourself if need be, and should easily find expert breakdowns on how the voice works from an anatomical standpoint. My training language speaks to the layman, using self-explanatory terms.

As a supplement to your training, I suggest you have at hand a means of recording yourself as you practice. Self-recording will help you monitor your progress and hear the reality of your voice. Your mobile phone or laptop, for example, will have a decent sound recorder. Make use of it! I am a firm believer in the now-hear-it-back approach to vocal training. Newly developing singers are often unsure regarding what is vocally desirable and what is not. The Playback Approach will help the adviser single out and explain what works and what doesn't, singing-wise. The vocal adviser's principal teaching aim is to enhance strengths and eradicate weaknesses.

A singer should always be humble. There will still be room for improvement, no matter how good you think you are. Don't fall into the trap of believing you are the finished article, knowing all

THE SECRET TECHNIQUE REVEALED

there is to know. Karaoke singers are the usual suspects here; given lots of compliments and enthusiastic claps on the night, but away from the lush complimenting vocal effect and twirling lights, their voices far from cut the mustard. Brilliant singers are a rarity, so you are probably an average vocalist at best. Be receptive to learning and open to criticism; that's how you grow as a vocalist. A lot of singers take vocal lessons, not to learn something, but for validation. They want to hear that they don't really need lessons after all, as opposed to where they are lacking, etc. So their usual response is to be defensive or even dismissive. Lose your ego! Just because someone is not telling you what you want or expect to hear, it doesn't mean they don't know what they are talking about or that they are not credible. If someone tries to educate you about your singing through constructive criticism, your interest level should rise. You should look to take something away from what they are telling you rather than try to justify why you are right and they are wrong. Remember, there are levels to singing. There is a vast gulf between the Karaoke singer, for example, and the professional singer. So once again, be humble. The path to vocal greatness begins with humility.

Now, maybe you are a songwriter who occasionally sings the odd note or two but never really thought of yourself as a singer. I would advise you to give your singing voice a more prominent role in the configuration of your art. You might not think much of your singing, but others may see your voice differently. Don't shut your singing voice out. Bring it into the fold and remember that it can be a vital component of the songwriting process, bringing quality musical ideas and transitions to the fore while you are composing.

Regarding rapping, I have found that many budding rappers suffer from a one-dimensional vocal sound. Your rapping should have multiple layers, many facets to its makeup; being able to tap into higher emotional planes when necessary. To lift off! Like how the voices of Tupac, Jay Z and Naz, for example, build the momentum as the song goes on, giving the lyrics varying degrees of emotional edge, depth and reality rather than sticking to one dynamic. A great rap voice has colour and

INTRODUCTION

personality to it. This Manual will help you create fire with your rap voice, as opposed to mere glints.

On a realistic level, I should point out that we all have our limitations. Most singers, like myself, are average singers. We can't all be outstanding vocalists; that's just a simple reality. Stay in your lane and look to capitalise on your strong points. Do the best with what you have and be the best you can be with what you have, then it will boil down to whether people like your vocal sound or they don't; but it will never be down to singing ability. So know your strengths and sing accordingly. Don't feel less of a singer because your whistle or falsetto register is not up to par with your singing idol's whistle or falsetto register.

I have included case studies of famous singers at work. These case studies will aid your understanding of the concepts described in the various lessons.

It's important also for you to partake in the steps (as opposed to merely just reading stuff) as you go through the book, so everything makes total sense to you. Some things I say may not make total sense to you if you don't physically carry out what I am asking you to do, particularly regarding breathing. So I encourage you to try out the things I am suggesting to avoid any confusion. What may read or come across as impractical or illogical on paper is a different story when put into action in actual life.

To finish, I would like to say that the training advice in this manual will mostly differ from the training advice others offer. Some may even find some of the things I say to be controversial. There is a mountain of vocal training literature and media out there, and I do not doubt that much of it is beneficial in myriad ways. What I am offering you over most, is a complete comprehensive singing set-up, a carefully laid out method that is a blueprint for pop vocal success. I would never say my way is the only way, but merely another way. It is your responsibility to experiment with other approaches if you so desire. What one person says is right, another will say is wrong and vice versa. Every vocal training system will have its champions and its sceptics, so at the end of the day, it all boils down to what suits and best works for you.

LESSON 1
A SOLID SINGING FOUNDATION:
ESTABLISHING A **UNITED VOCAL FRONT**
EXPANDING YOUR VOCAL EDUCATION AND ADDING TO YOUR ARSENAL OF TECHNIQUES

> Beauty is truth and truth beauty, — that is all ye know on earth, and all ye need to know
>
> — Keats

When we speak of a singer as having a great vocal technique, we are primarily commenting on the singer's exceptional skill at singing. A great technique gives you control over your singing, allowing you to be in control of your voice at every turn. A master vocalist (or vocal technician) is someone who is always one step ahead of their vocal sound, knowing how their voice will unfold and air itself before they open their mouth to sing. The vocal technician calls the vocal shots; their voice never escapes their grasp or 'dictates' to them. The art of singing invariably evolves around having full control over your vocal sound; over the communication of your voice at all times.

A **Solid Singing Foundation** is a dependable voice support system that will help you unlock the full potential of your singing voice, affording you the technical capability to achieve an appealing vocal sound on your singing terms. It will afford you full control over your vocal sound. Your singing will abide by a corporation of technique disciplines that will form the nucleus of your vocal approach, guaranteeing you **Quality of Sound**.

Throughout this all-important first lesson, I will lay down the building blocks of your solid singing foundation. As we go through each lesson, we will expand your vocal education and add to your arsenal of techniques. Along the way, you will discover your singing voice in revealing new ways. In time, you will establish a **United Vocal Front**, meaning your solid singing foundation is working in union with your own technique contributions to forge an appealing vocal sound. So you don't

A SOLID SINGING FOUNDATION

have to follow the singing foundation I am offering you to the letter. Go with what works for you and leave aside what doesn't. Adapt things to suit your personal vocal needs if need be. See your united vocal front as your passport to vocal freedom, allowing you to take your voice to its peak and technically go wherever your talent permits.

In today's studio recording world, the singer, more than ever, gets spoiled for verse, chorus and bridge choice; having the luxury of being able to pick the best lines from a host of vocal takes. Digital technology has transformed the way we bring our lead vocal performance to the masses. We have undoubtedly become overly reliant on computer software to bring about our end product rather than purely vocal craft. But there is also the argument that if the tools are available, use them. Representing myself in the best vocal light possible is what it's all about, you may say. As long as the final product sounds great, what does it matter, right? I mean, it's not as if the listener is questioning whether or not I did the vocal in one take, is it?

So if your vocal technique is not up to scratch, you are not automatically ruled out as a recording artist because the editing software is there to bail you out. The problem is, you don't get to do any picking or choosing during a live performance; you get one shot to represent yourself in the best light possible. Every line, therefore, has to be on par and that's why possessing a good vocal technique is paramount. Remember, at some point you will be expected to sing live, that's inevitable, so you have to be prepared and ready! Don't get caught out!

We did not always have the luxury of hand-picking our vocals. Back in the day, you had to know your craft. There was no editing software to come to the rescue. Programs like Logic Pro X, Pro Tools and Nuendo did not exist. Singing in tune, for example, was entirely down to you. Pitch-correcting software like Autotune and Melodyne was decades away. The artist was solely responsible for every facet of their vocal performance. The onus was on you to capture the magic, to make your performance rock from beginning to end. Think of it like this: when you press the key of a piano or pluck a guitar string, the instrument is the one that makes the resulting sound, not you.

LESSON 1

You trigger the sound, but you don't determine the sound's quality. So a bad piano, for example, will sound bad, and a good piano will sound good, regardless. But when you open your mouth to sing, you are the player and instrument rolled into one. Everything depends on you—the production of the sound and the quality of the sound. Without the aid of multi-tracking or computer software then, your only privilege was that you could go for as many takes as you like before settling on the one you felt to be the best of the bunch. So back then, having proper vocal technique was vital to being a successful recording artist. One glaring slip-up or blunder could cost you what would otherwise have been a great vocal take, and you would have to do the take all over again. Your game plan in the studio, therefore, was to go after the elusive magic take. An overall performance that ticked all the boxes, working on all levels.

Elvis Presley made his band record 31 takes of the song Hound Dog, over several hours, until finally satisfied with the right version. Version 28 was his eventual choice.[1] That must have been some session! How do you think you would fare in Elvis's shoes? To deliver a high standard, over and over, along with maintaining a ready, willing and able voice. To have recorded 31 takes of a frisky uptempo song like Hound dog over many hours, Elvis must have possessed excellent vocal technique, or a **Vocal Breakdown** would have ground him to a singing halt!

A Vocal Breakdown is usually a result of **Vocal Cord Exertion**, whereby the singer puts undue stress on their vocal cords. Singing without a method (without a proper technique behind your voice) leaves you open to vocal cord exertion, which is a detriment to vocal longevity. Be able to go the distance, whether you are performing live on stage or in a scheduled recording session. Proper technique is all-important to vocal longevity and being studio or stage productive.

A telltale sign of an encroaching vocal breakdown is when your voice feels highly uncomfortable, pressured or bothered. And if you persist in singing negligently, your voice shuts down on you.

---

[1] Hound Dog: 10 facts about Elvis Presley's hit song by Martin Chilton

A SOLID SINGING FOUNDATION

If your voice feels highly uncomfortable, let's say after two takes of a song, your vocal technique is in question. Meaning you are not going about your singing in the best technical way. It is your responsibility to look after your most prized asset, namely your voice. Before two boxers fight, a referee tells them: protect yourself at all times. You, the singer, must protect your voice at all times; when you are singing and when you are not singing. If you want a long-lasting voice, look after it! If you keep recklessly banging away at the keys of a piano, for example, those keys won't last very long, will they? You risk damaging them and putting the piano out of action. Handle your voice with the upmost care. At the core of any good vocal technique should be a 'voice protection first' mindset, which is also crucial for vocal longevity on stage or in the studio.

A proper vocal technique is a must if you wish to reproduce the sound you hear in your head into a digital print; in the same way a camera converts an image into a photo. What the camera sees, it captures with little to no compromise. Yes, there may be discrepancies relating to lighting and colour reproduction, etc. but you get as close to how the real thing would look, as seen by your own eyes, as is possible. In the same way, your vocal lines should practically be on target every time, sounding how you expect and intend them to sound, with next to no compromise. Your vocals, therefore, should tally with your **Sound Expectation.** It is via an effective technique that you will successfully meet your sound expectation. A great singer, as I like to say, is the equivalent of an expensive quality camera. The reproduction aspect will be spot-on nine times out of ten.

Now, let's say you record some vocals, and upon playback, some lines do not meet your sound expectation; so parts of your recording don't sound as you hoped or expected. Perhaps you could not capture the nuances a particular line required, or perhaps you could not get across the right flavour of emotion. Poor focus could be a significant factor here, but the likely culprit is poor vocal technique. If your vocal lines don't live up to your sound expectation, then your vocal approach is not in compliance with your singing. A quality technique invariably

LESSON 1

affords **Precision Communication**, allowing your voice to communicate in the exact manner it so wishes.

Now, although an excellent technique is necessary for a successful singing voice, you will want to mask your technique's contribution. You don't want your technique to impose on your vocal sound. Your technique takes its cue from you, not the other way round. Remember, emotion and feeling first, technique second. We can say the same regarding your voice training; your voice training should never display itself in your singing. You get this sometimes with pop singers, whose approach to singing scales crosses over into their approach to singing a song. So their vocal sound carries the **scale effect**— rigid in outlook and lacking that all-important naturalness of sound. Also, a lot of singers (including vocal coaches) fall victim to 'vocal correctness'. So their gallery of expertise takes hold of their singing, resulting in a textbook vocal sound. The method, therefore, is dictating to the voice, rather than being firmly in the background; and again, that naturalness of sound suffers, leaving you with soulless vocals.

The Breathing Enigma

I cannot stress enough the importance of correct breathing. When you breathe right, you sing right. Successful breath management is critical to successful singing. Control over your breath equates to control over your art. When you understand the nature of your breath, you deepen your understanding of your voice overall. Proper breathing technique promotes better diction and better quality of tone; also affording you a healthy and sustainable singing voice. The pivotal component of quality singing is quality breathing. The training in this key lesson will help shatter the Breathing Enigma. This Lesson applies to rappers in a big way. Without further ado then, let's get started. We will begin with the first steps of installing your Solid Singing Foundation.

A SOLID SINGING FOUNDATION

Vocal Start-Up—3 in 1 singing action

To set your Solid Singing Foundation in motion and to activate your technique, we will do a **Vocal Start-Up**. A vocal start-up occurs whenever you fill your stomach with air before you sing. I want you to perceive your stomach as being the hub of your vocal activities. Now, before we go ahead, do your best to avoid slouching, which is likely if you opt to sing seated. Let your torso gear towards being upright and aligned, to further assist your breathing and to support your singing overall. So here your chest can be a little forward and your shoulders a little back. Stay relaxed and focused throughout.

Now I want you to open your mouth and take in a comfortable amount of air promptly and directly to your stomach. Feel your stomach immediately shoot outward the moment you do so. The rest of your body should remain motionless as you do this. Only your lips and stomach move here, nothing else. Retain the air inside your belly for a few seconds before releasing it in one go. Feel your stomach collapse as you do so. The air you take in must go directly down to your gut in an instant, regardless of air quantity. So whether you take in a small batch of air or a large batch of air, it's an immediate, swift process. Optionally, you can assist bringing the air to your stomach by actively nudging your belly a little forward at the same time as you open your mouth to pull in air. Such action can enable speedier and more efficient air consumption. See your stomach as being **Air-Extended** once you fill it with air.

Note that the opening of your mouth, the intake of air and your stomach shooting outward, is a single simultaneously occurring split-second act. A 3 in 1 singing action. So the moment your mouth opens, your belly should already contain your desired amount of air. So you are consuming a batch of air in one swoop, as opposed to filling up your tummy by inhaling. Providing there is enough time or space to do so, you can casually inhale air leading up to where you plan to sing the next vocal line if you so wish.

You can also experiment with consuming air via your nose or varying the use of both options (mouth and nose) as you sing.

LESSON 1

So via your mouth for some lines, and via your nose for others; mixing things up, so to speak. As long as your nasal passages are fully clear, it is more than acceptable to consume air through your nose. One benefit of doing so is that you can deter early mouth or throat dryness. Sometimes breathing only through the mouth for long periods can lead to undesirable mouth or throat dryness, even more so when no water is at hand. Remember, if your nasal passages are not fully clear when consuming air through your nose, you may affect your ability to consume air quietly and speedily.

Another interesting breathing approach is to consume air through your mouth and nose concurrently. It's such things that amount to a technique particular or unique to you. Go with what breathing approach or scheme suits you and with what you find most comfortable.

Note that whenever you breathe directly to your stomach, your diaphragm contracts and your belly expands, filling with air as do your lungs. So your diaphragm and lungs naturally play a 'silent' but important role in things. Note also that once you take the air to your stomach and sing, you 'breathe' like you ordinarily would when you are talking, emitting imperceptible breath through your nose and mouth. Concerning your regular breathing, your singing should always have the same sensation as when you are talking. So you are simply replacing singing with talking. Nothing regarding your regular breathing should feel any different from it normally would do having launched your technique. So you are never going against the natural breathing order of things! You can see it all as a three-part process. You take the air in first, followed by singing, whereupon you breathe as you normally would do in everyday life. Once you set your technique in motion focus on your singing and let your 'natural breathing' take care of itself.

The next step will be to in incorporate the Secret Technique with your vocal start-up. I will discuss the secret technique later in this lesson.

The vocal start-up is an essential component of your solid singing foundation.

A SOLID SINGING FOUNDATION

Pure or Breathy?

Your singing palette has a choice of two distinct notes. A pure note or breathy note. A pure note comes as it is and will have no hint or trace of breath about it. In contrast, a breathy note will entail an obvious light or heavy use of breath, depending on which effect you are going after.

Now let's follow your vocal start-up with some pure notes. So, you will repeat the fundamentals as described earlier, only this time you will add sound. So the moment you feel your desired amount of air hit your stomach, follow through immediately with some vocals.

The next step is to sing some breathy notes. If you are a beginner or have never incorporated breathy notes in your singing, you may find this to be a tricky process at first. Practice the following Sigh Sound Exercise to get you into the swing of things.

Consume air to your stomach in the manner I have taught you and produce an exaggerated sigh. Feel your stomach wind down as the air escapes through your mouth. So your sigh, your collapsing stomach and release of air all occur at the same time. Program your sigh to be ultra breathy by consciously setting out to invade your sigh with air as it emits from your mouth. Have a sense of managing and being in control of the air breakdown as it takes place. Once you have got a feel for all of this, replace the sigh with a breathy note. So you will release the air from your stomach (allow your stomach to wind down) the moment you begin to sound your note. Progress to singing a breathy vocal line. So here you will time your stomach's collapse to cover the length of your vocal line with sufficient breath. Experiment with varying degrees of breath coating. So play with light and heavy breath usage. When producing heavily breathy notes, you can see yourself as 'blowing into a horn'. As if your voice is a wind instrument emitting your notes.

Try your hand at breathy vibrato. Hear examples of pure vibrato and breathy vibrato in case studies 1 and 2 (found at the

LESSON 1

end of this lesson). Here are definitions of **Vibrato** by three different dictionaries.

> A slightly tremulous effect imparted to vocal or instrumental tone for added warmth and expressiveness by slight and rapid variations in pitch — *Merriam-Webster*
>
> Vibrato is a rapidly repeated slight change in the pitch of a musical note. Singers and musicians use vibrato to make the music sound more emotional — *Collins*
>
> A repeated slight shaking in a musical note, either when played on an instrument or sung, that gives a fuller sound to the note — *Cambridge*

Breathy Note Mentality

The breathy note is largely unaccounted for in the pop vocal arena, seldom getting a look-in on modern-day record releases. Here I am talking about notes that are obviously breathy as opposed to being imperceptible. Having an unimposing thin lining of air to their makeup, for example. The pure note inevitably dominates the show because unlike a jazz singer, for example, the vast majority of pop singers sing without a **breathy note mentality**. So the idea of mixing pure and breathy notes in the same vocal line will not figure on their vocal radar. Another reason you rarely hear full-on breathy notes is many singers plain lack the technique to implement such notes.

 To create potentially exciting vocal lines, a singer needs every resource at their disposal. You should be able to go down or explore any avenue as you are creating music. The breathy avenue, therefore, should always be available to you. Subtle degrees of breath usage lie at the heart of the pro-vocal sound. It will mostly be an occasional here and there, light use of breath—unless we are talking about a breathy-based singer that

A SOLID SINGING FOUNDATION

is—but the 'heavy option' (marked use of breath) is always on standby if the singer feels so inclined.

The pro singer will understand the rich, telling nature of breath when appropriately applied, and will appreciate its musical potential regarding vocal line interpretation. The pro singer will see the value in juxtaposing pure and breathy notes in the same vocal line (dynamic line approach), and in presenting a particular line or sole lyric with an obvious breathy coating.

Make it your singing business to sing breathy notes at will if you so desire. Consider it a chink in your vocal armour if you lack the technical capability to paint your notes with breath. If your performance doesn't include breathy notes, it should not be because you don't know how to create such notes. A great technique is an all-encompassing one. Explore your breathy side and push the boundaries of your technique along with your vocal artistry. A well-timed breathy note can sometimes transform what would otherwise have been a run-of-the-mill vocal line into a standout vocal line instead.

Ask yourself the following question: when was the last time I sang a breathy note? If your mind went blank, then you are most probably in need of a breathy note mentality!

Breathy note mentality is an essential component of your solid singing foundation.

Discreet Air Consumption

The act of consuming air to your stomach is something you must do smoothly and inconspicuously. You should barely hear the air entering your body, if at all, and the listener should be none the wiser to your doing so. So your demeanour should give nothing away unless you intend it too. You should appear as normal; as if nothing is even going on. And this goes across the singing board. For example, some singers are prone to facial contortions, or roving eyebrows while they are entertaining. Eliminate that which distracts from your performance. Practising in front of a mirror will aid you here.

LESSON 1

Discreet air consumption is a **Covert Technique**. Meaning a technique that takes place behind the scenes and which only you are aware of. So you mask the inner workings of your technique from the listener. I will point out other covert techniques as we work our way through the manual.

Discreet air consumption can help counter mouth or throat dryness, promoting vocal longevity, as you'll be taking in the air quietly, hence smoothly. In contrast, if you were consuming air in a non-methodical offhand way the flow of air would not be as smooth hence leading to dryness. By implementing discreet air consumption, you are operating in voice protection mode.

Some singers have a habit of revealing their breath intakes; something a quality microphone will gladly highlight. If you hear a singer's breathing, it should be because the singer wants you to hear their breathing. If someone has pointed out to you that your breath intakes are too noisy, then you need to think about making some refinements or adjustments to your breathing technique.

Yes, breath intakes go hand in hand with singing, and there will be times when your breath intakes (for the sake of continuity and flow) will be audible on your recordings. What I am talking about here are breath intakes that are obtrusive and distracting, that detract from your performance. Aim to tame the volume of any air you take in or let out. Loud breath intakes point to suspect vocal or microphone technique. With a little practice, you'll find that it's relatively easy to take in air quietly. When you are singing, be breath-noise conscious; even more so when you are in front of a condenser microphone.

Note, sometimes an audible breath intake can add emotional content to a vocal line. So here the breath serves an artistic purpose, warranting its inclusion. So if there is a valid reason behind your audible breath intake, and you deliberately made it so, that's perfectly fine.

Discreet air consumption is part and parcel of good vocal or microphone technique and is an essential component of your solid singing foundation.

A SOLID SINGING FOUNDATION

Juxtaposition Mentality

Along with having a breathy note mentality, the singer will also have a **Juxtaposition Mentality**. The two mentalities go hand in hand. The Google description of the term Juxtaposition is.

> The fact of two things being seen or placed close together with contrasting effect. (In our case, the fact of two things being *heard* or placed close together with contrasting effect.)

So any significant play on contrast equates to juxtaposition, hence there are many variables. Singing a pure note or group of pure notes followed by a breathy note or group of breathy notes and vice versa is standard **Vocal Juxtaposition**. Further examples of vocal juxtaposition are singing low one moment and high the next and vice versa, or singing falsetto one moment and in your middle voice the next and vice versa. So you are adding spice to your musical content by juxtaposing different vocal elements for emotional effect.

Vocal Juxtaposition can be as diverse as you want to make it. A single line can have an array of vocal elements at work. It is through vocal juxtaposition that the vocalist gets to show his or her adventurous side. You can use light, or heavy degrees of vocal juxtaposition, depending on your vocal style. Michael Jackson is an example of a singer who uses vocal juxtaposition heavily. Shown in case studies 1 and 2, found at the end of this lesson.

Vocal juxtaposition is an essential component of your solid singing foundation.

LESSON 1

Levelled Singing

When we sing, we give little thought to the status of our chin. Is your chin 'sitting up' (away from the rim of the chest) or is your chin 'sitting down' (in line with the rim of our chest). What you want here is for your chin to be sitting down, which is representative of a level chin status.

Keeping your chin level and mostly stationary while you sing is the basis of **Levelled Singing**. Levelled singing requires focus and, above all, discipline. It's all too easy to forget to keep your chin in check, especially when you are in the zone. Even an experienced Levelled singer can get caught out sometimes and find they have been singing without a levelled chin without realising.

A common beginner mistake is lifting the chin when going for higher notes and dipping the chin when going for lower notes. Practise keeping your chin level at all times regardless of pitch. See yourself as observing an imaginary line running across the rim of your chest. Keep your chin 'central' (in line with the line) as opposed to above or below the line. Levelled singing will help safeguard your voice from vocal breakdowns while promoting vocal longevity hence productivity. By implementing levelled singing, you are operating in voice protection mode.

What I have given you here is more or less standard advice primarily aimed at the singer when in a studio recording setting.

Levelled Singing is an essential component of your solid singing foundation.

The Secret Technique

Of all the things you will learn from this manual, the aptly titled Secret Technique is the most powerful. In a nutshell, always have air inside your stomach while you are singing.

This rule only applies when singing vocal lines consisting solely of pure notes. Breathy vocal lines or lines that have a mixture of breathy and pure notes are another matter, as you would use the air in your stomach to help bring about such lines. So in such scenarios, you will use some or all of the air in your stomach.

Vocal coaches often say things like 'breathe to your stomach', etc. but you never hear them talk of holding on to the consumed air and keeping it present in your stomach while you are singing.

So what advantage is there to having air in your stomach while you sing, you may wonder? How does doing so benefit me? Well, the first thing to understand is that the air in your stomach will assist your every vocal move, supporting the production of your vocal sound. You can see your voice as perching atop of this multipurpose pillar of air, feeding off its fuel.

A big plus for having air in your stomach while you sing is that you can easily coat your notes with breath if you so desire. Most important of all, having air in your stomach while you sing promotes the crucial act of 'singing from your stomach'. I will discuss the act of singing from your stomach in lesson 6.

See the air in your stomach as being your source of power; your power supply. When you are filling your stomach with air, think of it as charging yourself up. And just like a mobile phone, etc. you will be at your performance-best when fully charged. Now let's go into a few details.

So, having done your vocal start-up and consumed your desired amount of air to your stomach, you will keep hold of the consumed air for the duration of the line you will sing, providing the line comprises pure notes only. Anything from a single lyric upwards can represent a line. Once you have finished singing the line, you can either allow your stomach to normalise (be empty of air), Option 1, or you can top-up (add further air to the existing air in your stomach), Option 2. Option 1 is the standard way to go and here you will do a fresh vocal start-up (refill your tummy with air) to sing the succeeding line. Option 2 only comes into effect when the succeeding line quickly follows and whereby you don't feel you have adequate time or space to normalise (a split-second apart, let's say). In most tight space situations your vocal start-up technique should stand you in

LESSON 1

good stead, as it will enable you to take in a sizeable amount of air swiftly during a tight window of space if needed.

From a technical standpoint, what you are aiming for at the conclusion of each line you sing is an air-intact stomach:. Meaning a stomach with as much original air intact as is possible and practical. Be mindful of your **Air Status**. You want a good amount of air present to help secure your foundation's structure, avoiding singing on an empty tank (with no air in your stomach). Air management is all-important. You should always be in tune with how much air you are taking in or releasing when you are singing. If you do find yourself singing on an empty tank, then you have failed to uphold your structure, i.e., you have unwittingly allowed yourself to run out of air. Lack of focus is the chief blame factor along with insufficient air consumption. To help yourself stay air-intact and prevent structure breakdown, it's important to consume sufficient amounts of air to cover your vocal lines; more so if you are about to sing a line jam-packed with lyrics.

Remember also, you don't have to wait until a vocal line's conclusion before topping-up. So if you arrive at a pause midway through singing a line, for example, you can, for whatever reason, consume more air.

Note that at no stage when utilising the secret technique are you holding your breath! You should never feel as if you are holding your breath or experience being short of breath while using the secret technique. You are comfortably keeping a batch of air in your stomach while you sing, nothing more. So as stated earlier, the moment you arrive at a pause is the moment you can either empty yourself of air or add additional air to your existing air. If you don't do one of these two options, then you are, in theory, holding your breath, which goes against your singing protocol.

If you recall what I said in the Vocal Start-Up section of this lesson: 'once you set your technique in motion focus on your singing and let your natural breathing take care of itself'. This advice also applies here. So even though you have gone one step further and are now holding air in your stomach, 'nothing regarding your regular breathing should feel any different from

A SOLID SINGING FOUNDATION

it normally would do having launched your technique. So you are never going against the natural breathing order of things!'

Remember that you have the option to consume the air slowly (through inhalation) if the time and space are available to do so. So if your next line is a few seconds from coming, you can opt to inhale air leading up to where you resume singing again. Or, you can stick with the standard approach and do a vocal start-up the moment before you resume singing again. The choice is yours.

Let's do another take on things for good measure. So, before every line you sing, take some air to your tummy. Retain this air in your tummy as you sing the line. The exception to this Retaining the Air rule is if the line includes breathy notes. Always aim to consume a larger quantity of air than usual if you are about to sing a *long* line or a line that will contain breathy notes. You can consider a long line as a line that consists of more than six lyrics. Assuming you have practised the song and know its particulars inside out, your Secret Technique should operate smoothly. So your vocal approach regarding each line is worked out beforehand. If you are singing off the cuff you will more or less play it by air. *Weighing up* each line as each line comes your way. So you will make *calculated* decisions on the fly regarding line length and whether to include breathy notes.

Now, although I told you to take some air to your tummy before every line you sing, you will occasionally encounter lines that follow one another in quick succession. Meaning you have a limited window of space to consume air on your preferred terms. In such tight space scenarios, your technique must be fully awake. Here you will want to bring air to your tummy speedily. So your vocal start-up and its 3 in 1 singing action will stand you in good stead here. Remember, no matter how tight the space, there should, in theory, always be an opportunity to take in some air, even if you have to *create* the opportunity yourself.

One of your more important roles as a performing singer (as well as a fundamental of your technique) is to look for or create opportunities too quickly and discreetly bring *supportive air* to your tummy before singing the line that follows. So you are

LESSON 1

setting up the next line to channel from your tummy hence successfully delivering it on all communicative levels. For example, the air supports your tone along with Vocal Longevity (helping to stave off fatigue). The air can enable you to have greater control over the singing of the line overall. Helping you to sing with authority and to easily sing with power if needed.

Keep your shoulders relaxed and a tad back with your chest a little forward to assist your air intakes as well as instil good vocal technique. Be mindful of your Chin Status also. Nothing gives a vocalist more singing security than to be armed with a reliable technique. Your technique is your rock!

Now let's move on to mixing pure and breathy notes in the same vocal line, which calls for a somewhat different approach, as here you will relinquish air to produce your breathy notes. There are two basic singing scenarios—going from pure to breathy or going from breathy to pure.

If you start off singing a line pure and want to finish the line breathy, allow your stomach to wind down (collapse into normalisation) as you engineer your breathy notes. So you oversee the release of the air, being in control of your stomach's breakdown throughout. Here is an example of a vocal line that starts pure and ends breathy. When transitioning from pure to breathy, perform the line legato. In a flowing seamless manner. Improvise your own melody. I have highlighted the breathy part in bold.

Yes it's true **I love you**

You can try singing a more advanced version of the same line when you feel ready to do so. Going from pure to breathy to pure.

Yes it's true **I love** you

A SOLID SINGING FOUNDATION

So here you will release air from your stomach to sing 'I love', continuing to sing 'you' as your stomach completes its wind down.

If you start off singing a line breathy and want to finish the line pure, use the air in your stomach to produce the breathy part; continuing singing the pure part as your stomach completes its wind down. You can never go wrong with consuming a decent amount of air before you sing a line that starts off breathy.

So you'll have an empty tank upon concluding the line, whereupon you will do a fresh vocal start-up; refilling your stomach with a new batch of air along with re-establishing your solid singing foundation. When transitioning from breathy to pure, perform the line legato. Improvise your own melody.

Yes it's true I love you

You can try singing a more advanced version of the same line when you feel ready to do so. Going from breathy to pure to breathy.

Yes it's true I love **you**

So here you will use a portion of the air in your stomach to sing 'yes it's true', saving some air to sing the concluding 'you'. You will want to consume a sizeable batch of air before attempting this line.

In time, the secret technique will become second nature to you. You will become highly receptive to consuming air; making sure your tank is never short of fuel. And you will reach the level where you will gauge your intake of air according to line length, and whether or not the line will include breathy notes. The secret technique may feel somewhat strange at first because you are doing something that will be entirely new to you; something altogether radical, I might say. But stick with it and the rewards will be considerable.

LESSON 1

The secret technique is an essential component of your solid singing foundation.

Lung Training Discipline

To finish off this lesson, I would like to share with you a workout I devised for increasing lung capacity, power and stamina.

As you should know your lungs are an important part of the singing process. Doing this workout daily will train you to consume significant quantities of air over set periods. Your breath control, timing and coordination will also benefit. This workout will do wonders for your secret technique.

To correctly do this workout, you will need access to a digital clock displaying a seconds counter. I like to do this exercise seated in front of my Apple laptop, keeping my eyes on the climbing seconds of the digital clock in the upper menu bar. Use whatever media device is most suited to you.

I want you to continuously inhale air directly to your stomach in cycles of 10-seconds at a time. If this already sounds too diverse or challenging for you for whatever reason, then do not feel obliged to take part. You can skip this exercise altogether. With that said, let's proceed.

Relax and focus. Look at the climbing seconds of your digital clock as they count upwards in banks of 10. Whenever 00 comes around to start a new minute, begin the workout by steadily inhaling air through your mouth directly to your stomach. So you will inhale air non-stop for 10-seconds straight at a time. Feel your stomach and sides expand as the air slowly floods into you. You are charging yourself up; filling your stomach with singing fuel. The incoming air should be free-flowing and devoid of hesitation. Keep your shoulders flat and your chin level. Draw the air in cleanly and discreetly. Have a grand sense of being in control of proceedings. Your chest should naturally puff out as you inhale. Aim your suction into the centre of your chest. When you see the number 0 appear,

A SOLID SINGING FOUNDATION

release all the gathered air in one go, and instantly repeat the process upon seeing the number 1 that follows.

So you are releasing all the air in one go on the appearance of 0 and inhaling again on the appearance of 1, until you see the next 0 come around whereby you will repeat the process. Do not wait for the 0 to settle before releasing the air, or you will not have sufficient leeway to prepare your next bout of inhaling when the '1' quickly follows suit. So here your timing must be on the ball.

The moment the 0 appears is the moment you relinquish the air and begin your next 10-second cycle of inhaling.

Maintain your control and focus to see through your 10-seconds of inhaling comfortably and productively. Involve yourself in the process by purposefully counting off the seconds in your mind. Such action will motivate you to meet your 1 minute (6 banks of 10) target. Preserve your structure. You should never feel as if you are holding your breath while doing this training. Once your tummy has maxed out, it will feel airtight and solid. Consider yourself fully charged up with air whenever you fulfil your 10-second bank cycle.

As you carry out this training, I want you to home in on your diaphragm, which like your lungs, is also an important part of the singing process. Healthline.com explains the diaphragm as follows.

> The diaphragm is a thin skeletal muscle that sits at the base of the chest and separates the abdomen from the chest. It contracts and flattens when you inhale. This creates a vacuum effect that pulls air into the lungs. When you exhale, the diaphragm relaxes, and the air is pushed out of lungs.

Using this workout to increase lung capacity, power and stamina should be a gradual process. Ultimately, you are aiming to go beyond the 10-second cycle mark. The higher the cycle count, the more in control you'll need to be. Once you have thoroughly mastered banks of 10 seconds, you can move on to banks of 15 seconds. So four banks of 15 (one minute in total),

LESSON 1

in place of six banks of 10 (one minute in total). Banks of 15 are a big step-up, being very testing. Master one bank of 15 first, followed by two banks of 15 (30 seconds) followed by three banks of 15 (45 seconds). And then the big prize: four banks of 15, one minute in total.

We have explored much in this heavyweight first lesson where you were introduced to many exciting new terms. Over the ensuing lessons, we will continue to expand your vocal education and add to your arsenal of techniques. Your vocal renaissance has begun!

Case Study 1

Search iTunes for *Human nature*
performed by **Michael Jackson**

Now let's pass the microphone over to pop vocalist elite Michael Jackson, to give you modern examples of vocal juxtaposition and vibrato usage.

Michael triggers the intensity factor from the off, and it is special to hear how he dabs the odd note here and there with a sharp use of breath. Doing so sparingly but tellingly. You can feel the latent energy in between the lines. I have highlighted Michael's breathy notes in bold.

'**Look**ing out, **across** the night-time'. Note how Jackson splits the syllables of the lyric 'looking' into part breathy and part pure. '**City** winks a sleepless eye'. Note Jackson's use of pure vibrato when he sings the lyric 'eye'. '**Hear** her voice, shake my window, sweet seducing **sighs**'. Note Jackson's use of breathy vibrato when he sings the lyric 'sighs'.

Michael's vocal maintains the tension until the end, giving us more breathy treats along the way. Thrilling stuff.

Jackson's modernistic vocal approach is an instructive sound manual for aspiring singers to glean from.

A SOLID SINGING FOUNDATION

Case Study 2

Search iTunes for *She's out of my life* performed by **Michael Jackson**

I have chosen this track to show a modern vocalist's creative use of pure and breathy vibrato. Hear how Michael openly involves himself in the vocal lines; committing to every lyric he sings. The artist and the subject matter are compellingly at one. The intensity is palpable, and Jackson infuses the vocal lines with genuine heartfelt emotion. I have highlighted Michael's vibrato notes in bold.

'She's out of my **life**,' (breathy vibrato), 'she's out of my **life**,' (breathy vibrato), 'and I don't know whether to **laugh** (pure vibrato) or **cry**,'(pure vibrato), 'I don't know whether to live or **die**,' (pure vibrato), 'and it cuts like a **knife**,'(pure vibrato), 'She's out of my **life**,'(light use of pure vibrato).

Michael's vocal continues in the same vein, with dashes of vibrato here and there as he wears his heart on his sleeve. And what an incredible display of emotion on the song's final line.

LESSON 2

STARTING FROM IN THE MIDDLE:
TAKING A LOOK THROUGH THE MIDDLE TONE WINDOW

EXPANDING YOUR VOCAL EDUCATION AND ADDING TO YOUR ARSENAL OF TECHNIQUES

> The one who controls the centre, controls the entire game
>
> — chess saying

I want you to use your chest as a springboard for launching and propelling your vocal activities. As you deliver your vocals, seek to feel your chest playing a role in the production of your notes. Let your chest and throat work in tandem to trigger your vocal sound. See your chest and throat as being a single singing unit. Such technical action on your part will increase your vocal mass; lending volume, strength, weight and body to your vocal sound. When I talk of vocal mass I am referring to voice size. Whether your voice is a small voice or a big voice.

The concept of feeling your notes as transmitting or emanating from your chest is one of two singing endeavours that make up what I have termed **Centre Action**. The other endeavour involves pitching from the centre of your voice; meaning to sing in you **correct middle tone**. This is the concept of what I call **Vocal Centralisation**. When you set out from or program yourself to operate from 'your centre', the act of singing can work more in your favour.

It is in and around the middle tone range where most of our singing action usually takes place, with the low and high tone range being ventured into now and again. The exception here is if you are artistically opting for, or naturally have, a high or low singing voice. But regardless of pitch, your voice will still have a middle premise.

The concept of precision singing, i.e., singing in your correct middle tone, is important for two principal reasons. The first

STARTING FROM IN THE MIDDLE

principle reason is **Vocal Maximisation**: getting the most out of your vocal range and doing so comfortably. You want to shift easily from one voice type to the next. For example, from middle voice to high voice or from middle voice to low voice. To get the most out of your singing range (and to be a step ahead of your singing range) you have to locate your vocal starting point. Your vocal starting point will lie in your **Vocal Ease Zone**, existing within a window of two choice or ideal singing keys. The serious vocalist will take the time to find their ideal singing keys; they won't just run with the first singing key that pops up in their head or predetermined by a karaoke machine, for example.

Remember, you and your voice are an instrument, and just as a Clarinet, for example, plays in the key of B Flat, you too will best operate and function in a specific key(s). Every singing voice is unique unto itself. If you sing a Whitney Houston song, for example, you'll be in for a hard vocal time if you opt to match her chosen key, which will probably be less than ideal for your voice. One person's ideal singing key is more often than not another person's struggle key. Therefore, picking the right key for your voice is all-important, if you want to have a singing advantage when you take on a new song.

By picking the right key you instigate a natural singing environment for your voice, creating the conditions for **Ease of Sound**: making singing occur as easy as talking (struggle-free vocals). So your ideal key is one that should best reflect your voice as a musical tool, catering for you across the vocal board; helping you to sing without restrictions or limits. An average singer can go a long way by teaming up with their ideal singing key. Hitting higher notes will be a more manageable enterprise. Think of it like this: if you pitch too high to begin with, you limit how much higher you can go.

The second principal reason singing in your correct middle tone is important relates to the unique nature of tone itself, and the crucial role tone plays in the making of an original sounding singing voice. By investing in your correct middle tone you open the door to vocal sound exclusivity and originality because now your singing voice and talking voice are operating on the same

LESSON 2

pitch level—the coming together of two vocal parties. I refer to this as the **Vocal Merge**: speaking voice and singing voice integration.

So a question you should ask yourself is am I pitching from the centre of my voice? In other words, am I singing in my correct middle tone? The likely answer is no, you are not.

A lot of singers unknowingly neglect their natural singing tone. Train yourself to sing with a voice that reflects the tonal character of your speaking voice. A simple way to do this is to first say the lyrics aloud before you sing them. Doing so will help you quickly establish a vocal merge along with pinpointing your vocal starting point, which will probably be a few tones lower than what you're accustomed to singing. Aim to sing with the same pitch level as your speaking voice rather than singing above your speaking voice.

So you are staying closely connected to your speaking voice as you produce your notes, enabling its tonal character to filter through into your singing. View your correct middle tone as an extension of your natural speaking voice.

Developing or inexperienced singers will almost always pitch higher than is necessary. This is mainly because our natural singing instinct is to lift our voice when we sing to better get our voice across; to afford ourselves a bigger sense of clarity and overall vocal mass. The downside is that you are overlooking your natural singing tone and are probably utilising a tone design that does not best represent your voice as a singing entity. With practice, you will easily achieve vocal mass while operating in your correct middle tone, doing away with lifting your voice.

At this stage, your correct middle tone will probably be light-sounding and lacking in true presence. Aim to master singing in your extended speaking voice, i.e., your correct middle tone. Set out to develop your natural singing tone to where it carries true volume, strength, weight and body. Maintain staying grounded because you will probably feel inclined to lift your voice a few tones as singing in your correct middle tone takes some getting used to.

STARTING FROM IN THE MIDDLE

Now let me be the first to say here that you are not obliged to operate solely within the confines of your correct middle tone window. The foremost teaching of this lesson is awareness over anything else. Knowing what's on offer to you as a singer and making choices from a well-versed standpoint. By all means, pitch your voice outside of your correct middle tone if you ultimately feel that's the best way for you to represent a particular song tonally and if it has no real negative effect on your vocal maximisation, etc. The difference here is that you are pitching higher out of artistic and informed choice rather than vocal ignorance or unawareness. So you would have done your homework and weighed things up before opting to operate outside of your correct middle tone window; knowing what you are getting yourself into performance-wise. So any higher notes that lie ahead won't catch you out.

Singing in your correct middle tone will make for a more powerful sounding impact voice. (I will discuss the impact voice in lesson 8.) Singing in your correct middle tone will also afford you a throat-pleasing singing life, helping to promote vocal longevity and avoid vocal breakdowns. Here is a simple practice recommendation to help you nail down your correct middle tone.

Say the word '**hey**', five times over in speedy succession. When you arrive at the fifth 'hey', throw in a sustained singing note. So sing the 'hey' instead of saying the 'hey'. Your sustained singing note should mimic the sound-level and tonal character and makeup of the preceding spoken parts. You are trying to stay in touch with and on a par with your speaking voice as much as possible when you convert the fifth 'hey' into a sustained note.

Hey hey hey hey **heyyyy**

Singing in your correct middle tone is an essential component of your solid singing foundation.

Now let's inspect some high-level examples of correct middle tone usage.

LESSON 2

Case Study 3

Search the internet for ***Lady***
performed by **Teddy Pendergrass**
Live in London, February 1982 Hammersmith Odeon

Teddy begins his magical performance with a spoken introduction, setting the tone. As he sings the opening verses, light and heavy breath coating comes into play, and he will delicately balance his use of breath coating throughout his performance. Note how beautifully entwined his speaking voice is with his singing voice. A fine example of the vocal merge. When he sings the line, 'You have gone and made me such a fool', he tellingly stays within his correct middle tone window. Most singers would have exited their middle tone window here, but Teddy stays grounded with no loss of impact. It's only when he gets to the line, 'But in my eyes', does he dramatically shift gears, bringing his impact voice into the fold. *Lady* is a highly impressive vocal display from one of the greatest romantic ballad singers of all time. Teddy's strong manly voice has much to teach you regarding breath usage and middle tone window discipline.

Case Study 4

Search iTunes for ***Halo*** performed by **Beyonce**

Beyonce confidently showcases her evenly weighted correct middle tone from the outset. We get a lovely middle to lower dip (a fine example of vocal juxtaposition) on the last lyric of the fourth line: 'Didn't even make a sound' (low note). She later treats us to a classy middle to high note transition, as she builds the intensity—'I ain't never gonna shut you out' (high note). After the electrifying chorus plays out, she switches to her high

STARTING FROM IN THE MIDDLE

voice: 'hits me like a ray of sun' (sung high). Thereafter she continues singing with strength at the uppermost of her middle tone, continuously adding wood to the fire as she soars towards the finishing line.

Halo is a charismatic performance from an exciting female vocalist.

Case Study 5

Search iTunes for **Water under bridges**
performed by **Gregory Porter**

Gregory sings at the heart of his middle tone, as he sets this bittersweet love song in motion. His correct middle tone has a stirring, animated strength to it. Note his ease of sound; spoken-like in tone and manner, as though he is sitting before you and relating his experience: 'Somebody told me get over it'. This sophisticated performance is middle tone territory all the way. When Porter wants to change the vocal mood, he injects more strength to the line, as opposed to going higher or lower in tone. For example, the turning point line, 'Do you remember (sung with strength), the days we used to spend'. Porter incorporates these strength injections throughout his performance.

What this performance teaches us is that you can get the vocal job done staying exclusively in your correct middle tone window; that you can be emotionally dynamic without calling on higher tones.

LESSON 3

SINGING WITH YOUR MIND:

USING **FOCUS** AS A CREATIVE FORCE

EXPANDING YOUR VOCAL EDUCATION AND ADDING TO YOUR ARSENAL OF TECHNIQUES

> Your lead vocal performance should be a manifesto of cognitive reasoning and inspired decision-making

A level of focus should take place as you sing. Tune into your art as you are making it. Focus is a significant factor behind a strongly functioning technique and quality sounding vocal overall. I want you to sing with your mind. To think about what you are singing while you are singing about it; to fuse your mind with your vocal lines. When we interpret lyrics, we react to those lyrics by using our mind and voice to bring those lyrics to life. Focus equips you to deliver the lyrics to the best of your creative ability. Every line should get your full-on artistic blessing.

The advanced singer will more than likely have a mental connection to every vocal line that exits their mouth. In contrast, the developing singer will more than likely want in focus, their vocal lines lacking full involvement and commitment. When the mind and voice are working as one the artist becomes a creative singing force. Practice to listen to and 'hear' your voice while you are outputting it. Such action will help keep you connected to your vocals at all times. Focus will help you to pinpoint your vocal tone in a strong consistent manner if needed, particularly when you wish to create **Vocal Contrast**. For example 'lifting' your voice (singing higher) when repeating a particular line or section of a song you previously sung in a lower key.

The quality of focus can often dictate the quality of art. You want your vocal lines to arrive in the best artistic shape possible.

SINGING WITH YOUR MIND

The serious vocalist will inevitably go after **Purity of Sound**: the quest for vocal clarity. Focus, i.e., singing with your mind, lies at the heart of Purity of Sound. Purity of Sound is central to the things I will talk about in this lesson.

Remember this, a voice is only as good as the listener understands it. Every word you sing should be intelligible to the listener. Account for the listener at all times. The listener should be able to make out every word that leaves your mouth. Be mindful of diction (your style of enunciation) at all times. Good diction is critical to an appealing sounding voice. Never take pronunciation for granted. Avoid getting caught out by wrongly pronounced words. An attentive listener will quickly pick up on a mispronounced word. Rappers can get away with this, but singers won't.

Always scan studio recordings for potential mispronunciations. Prepare studio recording sessions beforehand by examining the song's lyrics and taking the time to review any words whose exact pronunciation you are unsure of. In your everyday speech you may mispronounce common words without being none the wiser, assuming you are pronouncing them correctly. And this mispronunciation crosses over into your singing.

Cover yourself thoroughly, pronunciation-wise, before entering the recording booth. It would be a shame to have to redo an overall good take of a vocal line because of suspect pronunciation. You can use the audio pronunciation option in the Google Dictionary to assist you with pronunciation. Note, mispronunciation is acceptable if knowingly done so and serves an artistic purpose.

Be on the alert for defective notes (duds) on your vocal recording. Duds notes are notes that lack clarity or are indistinct or weakly delivered. For example, they may sound muffled, mumbled, unintelligible, half-formed or barely audible. Dud notes can easily slip through the net, if you listen back too casually. The prime reason duds slip through the net is that we listen to our vocals with the preconceived notion that we have already served the notes efficiently. We get slack regarding zooming into the delivery of the notes looking for discrepancies. Another reason is that correctly sung notes will precede and

LESSON 3

follow the dud note, helping to mask or camouflage the dud note. The brain, therefore, will assimilate the line based on the whole rather than note by note, so the dud note gets by undetected or overlooked.

Your primary vocal plan is to sing clearly and cleanly. You are going after **Separation of Sound**: making sure every lyric you sing gets highlighted. Every lyric should be definable on its own merits. An excellent way to analyse your recorded vocals critically, is to mute any musical accompaniment. Your Vocals must stand up to scrutiny when heard soloed. Take care to tail off your words, comprehensively. For example, if you sang the word 'eyes', it is critical that the 's' comes through and does not get lost in translation. So you may hear only 'eye' rather than 'eyes' upon closer inspection. You can sometimes get away with it, as the listener's brain will fill in the missing 's' for you. But make a point of not letting such defects, no matter how minor, find their way on your finished product. Every word you sing should get your full attention. It's easy to take one-syllable words for granted. Words like *I, but, and, if, it, to, be,* and *the*, are some prime examples. Such words should always ring through and possess clarity.

Treat these incidental words with maximum respect. Also, consider the fact that some words sound very similar to other words. For example, the word 'mind' sounds identical to 'mine'. So here you would make a point of highlighting the 'd'; making the 'd' ring through. Note that you should not achieve careful diction at the expense of musical flow. Your vocal art should meet the need of both—diction and musical flow.

Another thing a singer has to be wary of are undesirable mouth noises, which can easily find their way on your recording if you are not attentive. Mouth noises can occur when your mouth shifts from one position to another as you go to sing the next word/line. Examples of mouth noises are *smacks* and *clicks,* which are usually a result of lower and upper lip contact or when the head of the tongue meets the roof of the mouth or upper teeth. An overly moist or dry mouth can be a contributory factor to mouth noises. A quality condenser

SINGING WITH YOUR MIND

microphone can sometimes highlight such anomalies to a vocal line's detriment.

Lets me look at an example of where a mouth noise could be possible. Sing the word 'around', stretching the tail of the word: Aroun**da**. Note when you execute the **da** part, the head of the tongue hits the roof of the mouth, which presses down on the tongue to produce the '**da**'. Now it is as your tongue leaves the roof of your mouth and your lips form the next word you wish to sing, where mouth anomalies such as smacking can occur. So it's as a shift/adjustment takes place, or when you want to take in air to sing something else, where you have to be mindful.

To avoid this, you sing the 'around' straight, with no stretch (**da**). This way, your tongue rests and it stays there, as opposed to lifting to sound the **da**, possibly creating a mouth anomaly thereafter.

Say-Singing

If a lyric is not ringing through (meaning it is lacking in clarity, definition or volume) you can Say-Sing the lyric in question. So here you are saying and singing the lyric in combination. So the moment you say the lyric you are already adding a singing tone to it, instantly converting the lyric into a musical note. Such action will afford the lyric more presence and intelligibility. Say-singing is a form of what I refer to as Covert Technique. So the fact you are say-singing should not be apparent to the listener. As you carry out say-singing, you are in effect masking your technique. Say-singing can also be effective for helping a vocal line get off on the right foot. Say-singing can also aid pronunciation. Never achieve Say-Singing at the expense of musical flow.

The act of singing is ultimately about decision-making. As we are singing, we are making quick, decisive decisions regarding technique usage and tone or lyric presentation. You must be at the helm of these decisions. Have a thought process going on while you are singing. And it is via this **vocal thinking action** that you invite your improvisational side to have a say in things.

LESSON 3

Singing with your mind will help you better balance your emotional outlay. Emotion is something you should weigh up as you sing. The pro singer, like an actor or actress, will account for emotion at all times; judging whether their use of emotion should be of a light, medium or heavy nature.

Singing with your mind promotes singing with precision: the voice, and the mind behind the voice, forming a unity and working in tandem.

Vocal Line Similitude

Vocal Line Similitude relates to upholding **Vocal Character Consistency**. To make your verses appealing to the listening ear, singing law naturally dictates that the vocal lines that make up your verses should have a uniform, orderly pattern of sound to their overall makeup. So you set the scene with a particular vocal character, and you stay consistent with that vocal character as you sing your way to the chorus. So you choose a 'colour scheme' and stick with it.

For example, you might go with a vocal character that displays a certain tone or manner of voice, for. Or a vocal character that develops around energy and urgency, or is laid-back or casual. Or you might approach the vocal lines in a certain rhythmical manner. Each fresh line you sing will be a reference to the line that preceded it. You maintain the character until you get to the bridge or chorus, whereupon you can show your adopted vocal character in another but closely related light. Listen to *I Have Nothing* by Whitney Houston for a first-rate example of vocal line similitude.

The pro singer will approach a Verse or chorus, etc. systematically or linearly, with an underlying, astutely formed uniformity. They will choose a harmonious colour scheme to tell their verse, bridge or chorus story and their voice will stay in character throughout as they do so. Vocal character consistency is a highly important facet of a recording voice.

A lot of what I have said in this lesson will not be critical to genres of Popular music such as death metal and hard punk, for example. Here the vocal is more about atmosphere and vibe,

SINGING WITH YOUR MIND

etc. rather than spot-on diction or enunciation and so forth. But being focused is still a crucial element. Singing with your mind still applies. The best death singers are champions of vocal line similitude.

Singing with your mind is an essential component of your solid singing foundation.

LESSON 4

SLOW THE WHOLE THING DOWN:
FOR A BETTER VOCAL SOUND

EXPANDING YOUR VOCAL EDUCATION AND ADDING TO YOUR ARSENAL OF TECHNIQUES

> You sing as if you are worried about missing the last train out of here

Rushing your vocal lines is something you may do but are unaware of doing so. When singing without musical accompaniment (a cappella) the uninitiated singer will needlessly hurry their vocal lines. Such action may be a disservice to your singing, especially in an audition setting. In extreme cases, the singer's vocal may be unintelligible. Nerves can be a contributory factor here, but the most likely reason for Line Rushing is a lack of vocal maturity and experience.

Slowing down your vocal lines can bring refinement to your singing and enhance how others hear and absorb your singing. When singing solo, remember that you dictate and control the pace. Pacing your vocals conveys authority and confidence. Hurried singing, if not done fittingly or artistically, will not meet the approval of the discerning ear. Savour the lyrics. Sing in your own comfortable time: **singing at ease**. Singing at Ease promotes vocal intelligibility. Your number one singing priority is for the listener to understand you comprehensively. You want to communicate a natural sounding, fuss-free voice; a tidy vocal sound.

A simple trick to help counter against Line Rushing is to listen to yourself as you sing. Such action will also help you present your vocals with sophistication and finesse, and to get the most out of your vocal output.

Note you are not dragging your lines out unnecessarily here. Your lines must appear as normal. Another example of Covert

SLOW THE WHOLE THING DOWN

Technique. So you are covertly pacing your lines for maximum effectiveness.

You can regard singing as musical recitation. See yourself as being a narrator or storyteller. When someone is relaying a story, they do so at an intelligible, steady pace. If they were hurriedly conveying the story, would you derive any genuine enjoyment or entertainment from hearing it?

Note that rushing or speedily delivering your vocals is all very well if you are making an artistic point by doing so, and your doing so can emotionally touch the listener.

You can even get away with a lack of full intelligibility if you are making up for it in other ways, such as bringing atmosphere and vibe to the proceedings.

Slowing down your vocals sets the scene for singing with your mind; opening the door to Audiation: pre-hearing your approach to a vocal line or a particular note or set of notes within a vocal line. Your sense of time and space and how you go about using time and space will heighten.

Slowing down your vocals is also applicable to singing with musical accompaniment. So we are talking about your standard 4/4 Pop song here.

You should not achieve slowing things down at the expense of musical flow and sensibility.

Slowing down your vocals is an essential component of your solid singing foundation.

Case Study 6

Search iTunes for **Every Time We Say Goodbye**
performed by **Ella Fitzgerald**
This particular version is from her album
Ella Fitzgerald sings the Cole Porter songbook

Here is a fantastic example of a singer slowing the whole thing down. Note how the First Lady of Song is in total command of

LESSON 4

the lyrics from the off as she sings with her mind. Each line she delivers oozes with vocal authority. Fitzgerald allows the lines to breathe. Her vocal art begins and ends with giving every syllable the utmost attention and respect.

'Every time we say goodbye, I die a **little**.' Hear how diligently and classily she sings the lyric 'little'. She remains poised throughout, with impeccable elocution. Her clarity and cleanness of sound are in another league. Ella's phrasing and sense of time and space are spot-on as she slows the lines down to telling effect.

Listen carefully to her treatment of the chorus, in particular, the lines I have highlighted in bold.

'Why the gods above me, **who must be in the know** (slowed down), **think so little of me** (slowed down), they allow you to go.'

Here, ladies and gentlemen is song interpretation of the highest calibre. Ella's notes are unique little gifts to the discerning ear. Listen to fellow jazz songstress Sarah Vaughan (Sassy) for more of the same slowing things down magic.

LESSON 5

SINGING OUT: SINGING WITH THE 4 C'S
CONFIDENCE, COMMITMENT CONVICTION AND CLARITY

EXPANDING YOUR VOCAL EDUCATION AND ADDING TO YOUR ARSENAL OF TECHNIQUES

> Sing out!
> If you want your vocals to count

To sing out or rap out means to present your vocals with confidence, commitment and conviction: the 3 C's. Your voice should be alive with self-belief as you express yourself musically. You may be shy by nature, but when you open your mouth to sing, all shyness should evaporate. Switch yourself on mentally and go into **Fearless Vocal Mode**. Project your voice! Singing judges will quickly pick up on any vocal uncertainty or doubt.

When you sing out, you are lifting the sound level of your voice to facilitate communicating your vocals in a clear, firm way. Broadcast your vocals outwards (to others) as opposed to singing inwards (to yourself). So you must endorse a forward and direct sound rather than an 'inward and indirect' sound.

Singing out will help counter dud notes and enhance diction and elocution. Singing out is like Sounding out, which plays a role in singing from your stomach. (I will discuss sounding out in lesson 6.)

The practice of singing out increases your sense and awareness of volume and how sound level affects your vocal sound. You will manage and control volume in a purposeful, balanced and artistic way as you output your vocals. You will tailor your vocal lines to meet a particular volume threshold if need be, while being conscious of 'breaking the barrier' for much loud moments. An Audio Limiter works similarly.

LESSON 5

As a singer, you are your own amplifier. You control every aspect of the sound you create. You can see your chest as being akin to a loudspeaker complete with a speaker grille. Let your volume cue from and emanate from your chest.

Singing out also involves **vocal weight distribution**: deciding whether to distribute your vocals in a light, medium or heavy voice.

Singing out promotes clarity of tone and of the lyrics you sing, and is an essential component of your Solid Singing Foundation.

Case Study 7

Search iTunes for *Honey Man Blues*
performed by **Bessie Smith**
Recorded October 25th, 1926 New York

Here is an excellent example of singing out, by none other than the Empress of the Blues: **Bessie Smith**. Although this recording dates back to the mid-1920s, what is at once apparent here is the clarity and immediacy of Smith's no-nonsense vocals. Each note projects like the chime of a church bell. There is a sober truth underlying Bessie's voice. A truth that knocks on your door and won't go away until you open up!

Case Study 8

Search iTunes for *Money Over Bullshit* performed by **Naz**

Now, for an outstanding example of Rapping out by a standout rapper: Naz. Note how Naz maintains vocal character consistency throughout. Note also how every lyric rings out, even when the vocal lines are jam-packed. You feel everything he says to you as each line impacts like a heavy punch. Naz raps with a thorough belief in his message, and he creates fire with his voice to ensure his message burns into your consciousness, waking you up!

LESSON 6
MAKING THE NOTES COME FROM YOUR STOMACH (AND NOT THROUGH YOUR NOSE):
FROM THE STOMACH ASSURANCE

EXPANDING YOUR VOCAL EDUCATION AND ADDING TO YOUR ARSENAL OF TECHNIQUES

> 'Sing from your stomach' said the teacher to the student.
> 'But how? My stomach doesn't have a voice box,' replied the student.

I wrote in lesson 1 that 'I want you to perceive your stomach as being the hub of your vocal activities'. I primarily said this because your vocal technique, as taught to you in this manual, actively begins and ends with your stomach. If you consciously involve your stomach in the production of your notes, then you are endorsing the act of singing from your stomach: meaning you are actively targeting your intakes of breath to go directly to your stomach to serve and have an input in your singing thereafter.

If you sound like you are singing through your nose rather than 'from your stomach', I would say there are two chief things you should look at. The first thing is your breathing technique or approach to breathing as you sing. Breath is the cornerstone of all vocal techniques. How you breathe, therefore, affects how you sing. So if you sound like you are singing through your nose, the relationship between your breathing and your stomach is probably not a harmonious one; lacking true union. Ask yourself these questions: are my breath intakes methodical and systematic or are they the opposite: unmethodical and unsystematic. Is my utilisation of breath directed or undirected?

To set yourself up to sing from your stomach, you first need to supply your stomach with air. Endorse what I refer to as a **Stomach Mindset** while you sing. Remember, your stomach is the hub of your vocal activities. Focus your breath intakes to go straight to your stomach as opposed to taking in air without a

LESSON 6

specific aim or purpose. The secret technique breathing technique system will stand you in good stead here. To give you an idea of what it feels like to sing from your stomach, or rather, have your stomach play a role in the note-making process, try the following practice recommendation:

I want you to mimic a yawn. Feel the air go directly to your stomach as you open your mouth to set your yawn in motion. The yawn sound you make will come directly from your belly. Exaggerate the yawn for added effect. Feel your stomach collapse as you let out your yawn sound. Move on to substituting the yawn for a sustained note. There is no better way of showing the concept of singing from the stomach than doing a programmed exaggerated yawn or sigh.

The second thing you should look at if you sound like you are singing through your nose are your nasal passages. You can easily replicate the singing in the nose sound effect by keeping your nose pinched while you endeavour to sing. What you hear is a blocked or closed sound as opposed to a more natural open sound. You can also describe what you hear as being nasal or whiny. So it stands to reason that if you sound like you are singing through your nose, then perhaps you have an issue of some kind regarding your nasal passages. So we can say some level of constriction is taking place which could also relate to your throat as well as your nasal passages. A lot of singers who sing through their nose are not aware of doing so. Usually, someone has to point this out to them before they get wise to the fact.

You mustn't confuse a nasal singing tone with nasal resonance here. The nasal resonator is one of the four vocal resonators; the mouth, chest and head being the other three. Some voice specialists argue that we need a little of the nasal sound for a balanced vocal production. So if we are to have a balance of resonance qualities, you will need some activation of the nasal resonator. Whether nasal resonance has applicability to a quality singing tone though is open to question.

Now, let me point out that there is nothing wrong with having a nasal vocal sound if, 1: you, the singer, know that you sound nasal and artistically endorse sounding so, and 2: your vocal

MAKING THE NOTES COME FROM YOUR STOMACH

sound is consistently nasal throughout, as opposed to being nasal in parts, which would undoubtedly point to a poor or suspect technique. So here your method of vocal production is working against you rather than with you. Note that if you naturally have a distinctly nasal sounding speaking voice, then it makes sense that your singing voice will reflect your speaking voice, also sounding nasal. In such cases, your nasal vocal sound has full justification and does not point to something being wrong. Our concern here is with random irregular nasalness rather than consistent nasalness or what we can cite as natural nasalness.

Outside of the two things I said you should look at (namely your breathing technique and your nasal passages), the consensus, from a voice science anatomy-based standpoint, is that a nasally vocal sound results from the soft palate not being lifted high enough as the singer is singing, which could apply to you. I say investigate your breathing technique or approach first followed by your nasal passages and if those things are not responsible, then at the very least you would have eliminated two probable causes.

Now let's delve deeper and discuss Stomach Activation and Sounding Out, which as a Cooperative, help to offer you **From The Stomach Assurance**.

Stomach Activation

The moment you intentionally fill your stomach with air is the moment **Stomach Activation** takes place. It's as simple as that! This is the first step to programming your notes to come from your stomach. So you are inviting your stomach to play a role in your singing from the get-go. As soon as you feel the air contact your stomach, consider yourself activated and ready to go. What you are essentially doing is establishing your foundation before you sing. You are not jumping in head-first, so to speak. You are entering the singing arena with solid back up. Whenever you refill your stomach with air, you are re-activating it: meaning you are maintaining your stomach's role

LESSON 6

in your singing. Having activated your stomach, the act of Sounding Out can enter the fold.

Sounding Out

Sounding Out is a covert vocal technique that helps you to channel your notes outwards (through the mouth), preventing them from going inwards (through the nose). You will achieve this by promoting quality diction along with a strong, consistent level of sound. You will be working the line, overseeing its delivery to ensure open-sounding notes as opposed to closed-sounding ones. So having activated your stomach, you don't rest on your vocal laurels, you make the line accountable to your stomach. You can see yourself as conditioning your notes to come from your stomach. To the listening ear, your singing appears as standard, but in reality, you are covertly using sounding out. An excellent way of understanding how sounding out, in theory, works, is to do the following suggestion. Record yourself if possible.

Pinch your nose and sing the line 'You're all I need'. Note that the phonetic nature of the word 'need' causes it to channel inward through the nose (closed in sound), in contrast to the other words, which channel outward through the mouth (open in sound). So now that you know the word 'need' will channel inward, perform the line again, only this time singing the word 'need' in an assertive, strong tone of voice, to help negate the nasal inward-going quality of the word. Notice that now you have attempted to channel the word 'need' outwards, the inward 'through the nose effect' gets much reduced if not all. Sounding out works along similar lines.

On a simple level, you can see sounding out as being an active 'sound manipulation mechanism', to ensure From The Stomach Assurance: meaning all the notes you sing are coming from your stomach. You can see yourself as being one step ahead of possible inward-going notes; securing their outward-going status.

Lesson 6 is an advanced singing lesson. Some of what I have discussed might be a little over your head at this stage. But I

MAKING THE NOTES COME FROM YOUR STOMACH

promise over time, as your awareness, voice and vocal technique grow, everything in this lesson will come to make sense to you.

LESSON 7

THROAT DISENGAGEMENT:
THE MAKING OF AN INDEPENDENT SINGING VOICE

EXPANDING YOUR VOCAL EDUCATION AND ADDING TO YOUR ARSENAL OF TECHNIQUES

> I won't be bringing my throat to the studio with me today if that's okay with you?

A throat-heavy vocal production is something developing pop singers invariably subscribe to without appreciating the fact that they can largely get by with little to no throat involvement at all.

So here the singer will emphasise the throat, rather than the actual voice itself, to trigger the majority of their notes, and will assume that doing so is a justifiable and warranted application if they are to best communicate their vocals. For example, they will assume that involving the throat is crucial for tagging their voice with the right emotion or feeling they wish to convey.

The fundamental problem with throat-heavy vocal production is that it can quickly wear down your voice (vocal cord exertion) and lead to a possible vocal breakdown after only singing a few songs, particularly if you involve high notes.

The golden rule in singing is to protect your voice at all times. Your singing mindset and technique should foremost centre around voice preservation.

Now, all I have said so far in this lesson only accounts for one side of the throat-heavy story. One could easily point out genres of popular music such as hard rock and heavy metal, for example, and say that a throat-heavy vocal production is more or less the standard. But not so fast. It's important to understand here that professional hard rock and heavy metal singers will have their voices covered from a voice preservation standpoint. They will be **Throat Conscious**: be in tune with

THROAT DISENGAGEMENT

their throat conduct at all times while they perform; supervising how their throat interacts with their vocals while they are singing. So there will be a method at work behind their vocal output, every step of the way. Sensible management of your throat conduct will ensure vocal longevity in the studio and on the stage.

The trick to their vocal art then is to use a clever combination of both parties: the throat and the singing voice. As they sing, they implement degrees of **Throat Disengagement**. And here we are talking about across-the-board throat disengagement, covering all voices: low, middle, high and impact voice. Usually, any calculated minimisation of the throat gets reserved for high or impact notes. Throat disengagement is a principled vocal technique that revolves around minimising or neutralising the use of your throat while you are singing. Your singing voice, therefore, will sound the note independently of the throat or with minimal throat usage. Throat disengagement will afford you an Independent Singing Voice: a voice that fully functions without excessive leaning on the throat.

I would like you to invest in (across-the-board) throat disengagement as part of your vocal technique. So you will train yourself to rely mostly on your singing voice itself to produce your notes rather than your throat. You will use your throat where and when applicable; selectively. Your throat usage will be method-based, monitored and controlled as opposed to your throat having free rein over your vocals, doing as it pleases. You will feel when your throat wants to get involved, and you will say to what degree you permit it to do so, if at all. You can see yourself as keeping your throat at bay until you permit it to get in on the act. Make your throat work in your vocal favour. Vocal preservation will lie at the heart of your vocal art—singing in a vocal cord-friendly way. Yes, there may be times when meeting your sound expectation will mean giving your throat full access. For example, performing a growl-like vocal effect, etc. Carry out any full-on throat usage with control and technique.

Throat disengagement is a crucial factor in the production of impact and sky notes. (I will discuss sky notes in lesson 8.)

LESSON 7

It is through throat disengagement that **Note Gliding** can come into play. Note gliding is whereby you 'glide' over a series of notes that form part of a vocal line. So you consciously and deliberately disengage your throat as you sing the series notes, doing so whether or not such action is warranted. Note gliding promotes vocal longevity, helping to keep your voice stress-free throughout a long live performance or recording session.

To get into the throat disengagement swing of things, experiment with humming higher or lower notes with your mouth firmly closed, pitching the hums with no throat involvement. So you are relying on nothing but your voice to sound your notes. This is also a great way to warm up your voice before a studio session. With focused application, Throat disengagement will quickly show its merits and will become second nature to your singing makeup. Never achieve throat disengagement at the expense of a natural-sounding vocal sound. Note that an altogether natural-sounding singing voice will always include degrees of throat usage.

Throat disengagement is an essential component of your Solid singing foundation.

Vocal Containment

You can see **Vocal Containment** as being an extension of Throat Disengagement. Vocal containment revolves around the monitoring and reduction of any mouth, lips, tongue and jawline movement as you sing. Yes, your mouth, lips, tongue and jawline will naturally be active as you sing, but by consciously implementing vocal containment, you will be far more aware of their movement than you usually would and will have a sense of taming and lessening such movement to some discernible degree. You will be at the forefront of any movement taking place in your vocal chain. The key point of vocal containment is to access higher levels of control while you are singing. Here are some vocal containment tips:

When utilising vocal containment do not widen your mouth unnecessarily. See yourself as 'singing through a slit'. Your mouth should only be as open as it needs to be to create your

THROAT DISENGAGEMENT

desired vocal sound. Keep a relaxed tongue. Be conscious of your mouth or jawline opening and closing. Limit your lip movement as much as possible. I like to describe it as singing inside of your mouth.

Vocal Containment can encourage focused and streamlined vocal line delivery. See yourself as being at the fore of your vocal sound; as keeping a tight rein on your singing overall.

Vocal Containment can play a role in high or impact note production. Never achieve vocal containment at the expense of a natural-sounding vocal sound. Vocal containment is an optional (advanced) vocal approach.

LESSON 8
HEADING FOR THE SKY AND DIGGING DEEP:
THE **HIGHER** AND **LOWER** NOTE CONUNDRUM

EXPANDING YOUR VOCAL EDUCATION AND ADDING TO YOUR ARSENAL OF TECHNIQUES

> The moon looks just as beautiful in the river as it does up there

The **Sky note** tickles our musical fancy like no other kind of note; it simply allures and captivates us. A sky note is not your average (comfort-zone) high note, which should not pose a great deal of difficulty for a capable enough singer. Sky notes are more challenging to sing, existing higher up the scale and will more than likely give the unschooled vocalist a harder singing time if their technique is not up to par. A singer's ability to hit higher notes effortlessly is often the deciding factor regarding how accomplished we perceive them to be. For example, the unwritten consensus is that any diva worth her salt should be able to leave you entranced by her sky note prowess. A sky note usually signals a key or big moment in a song and tells you that the singer is tonally switching gears for emotional or dramatic effect. If you are a singer who favours sky notes or even falsetto or whistle notes, this means of vocally expressing yourself, will usually play a big part in defining your vocal sound—being your vocal calling card. Think Mariah Carey, Minnie Ripperton and Johnnie Wilder Jnr (lead singer of Heatwave).

Once you venture beyond your upper-middle tone, you will comfortably sing high until a certain point. Beyond that point is what I refer to as your **Sky Zone**, and it is when the developing singer sets foot in their sky zone that they usually experience singing problems. For example, their voice may go into disarray

HEADING FOR THE SKY AND DIGGING DEEP

or crack when going for non-standard high notes. Not every singer is fortunate enough to have a multi-octave range. The fact is, most popular singers have a limited vocal range, though you usually find that if you are weak in one area, you become stronger in another. So if, for example, you have a comparatively limited vocal range, you can compensate for this shortcoming by combining nuanced phrasing with emotional immediacy. Know your limitations and play to your strengths. With practice and the correct vocal approach, you will extend the range of your voice by a few notes at the very least, if not much more. So you will experience some level of sky zone success, depending on your talent. Sky notes are not a performance necessity but a performance asset. There have been many wonderful female vocal performances throughout pop history that stay in middle tone territory all the way, having no low notes on board.

A simple way to sing sky notes on your own terms is to lower the key of your chosen song to accommodate your voice as much as possible when you head for the sky. So you will give the impression of hitting sky notes but in reality, are hitting less challenging higher notes. So when you go higher, the listener takes it at face value. The higher notes they hear will not be as high as they assume. Note that if you are already mindful of your vocal starting-point and are singing in your correct middle tone and ideal singing key, then you are already winning the sky note battle.

Now if you want to face sky notes head-on having started singing a song outside of your correct middle tone window, then here are some proven technique tips:

I want you to perceive sky notes from an eye-level perspective, as notes sitting in wait directly in front of you as opposed to above you. Always be aware of your chin status when negotiating sky notes. Some singers are prone to lifting their chin (reaching) when going for higher notes. Do not feel you have to adjust bodily or make a point of doing something, in particular, to make the note occur. Be sure to have air inside your stomach as you create and produce your sky notes. The air will assist and support your vocals. Encourage centre action:

LESSON 8

feeling your high notes as transmitting from your chest along with your head. Put throat disengagement into full effect. You want to take your throat out of the equation here. It's important to feel in total control when producing sky notes, so vocal containment can also figure here. Focus is paramount when heading for the sky, so stay connected to your vocals throughout. You can also apply all these tips when creating falsetto and whistle voice notes. You can also experiment with producing your sky notes in a stylised voice, which can help you conceptualise sky notes with a different emotional flavour.

Stylised — done in a mannered and non-realistic style to create an artistic effect.

Strive to pre-hear your higher notes. In this sense, you are 'one step ahead of the note' which aids having control of the note's production. Remember, breath management can play a big part in successful higher note-making. You can use varying degrees of breath distribution (discernible and indiscernible) to carry out and bring about your higher notes. The same principles can also apply to lower note production.

As mentioned in the lesson on throat disengagement, when practising going up or down 'experiment with humming higher or lower notes with your mouth firmly closed, pitching the hums with no throat involvement. So you are relying on nothing but your voice to sound your notes'. Pre-hear the higher notes as you do so. Practice transitioning from one voice type to the next. For example, middle to high or middle to low or low to high or high to low. Pitch with freedom. Don't force the transitions, let them smoothly and easily occur of their own making, without you having to do anything in particular. See yourself as helping the process along more than anything else, as giving the transition a gentle 'nudge' as opposed to a forceful 'push' as you 'adjust' your voice to go from one tonal extreme to the other (for example, from low to high or vice versa). Output your voice in a light, unimposing manner as you carry through the transitions. You are lessening your throat's role in the note's

HEADING FOR THE SKY AND DIGGING DEEP

production and letting your voice itself independently execute the note. In time, as your voice gets stronger, your higher notes will gather in weight. Once again you can work with your breath. If you struggle with sky notes, then turn to your breath for the answers. Think in terms of upfront breath usage or background breath usage. With upfront breath usage you will allow your breath to play an active role in the note's production to whatever degree you feel fitting. So you will consciously implement breath in the making of your notes. Even your high pure notes can come across as sounding pure but have a tinge of quiet breath at their core. With background breath usage, your breath plays a supportive, 'backing up' role rather than a perceptible one; sitting at the foot of your notes through occupying your tummy. So here, your breath acts as a foundation over which your voice operates.

Digging Deep

As you dig deeper into the lower range of your voice, you will unearth the tonal gems that lie in wait for you there: we are talking about the **Bottom Note**. So captivated are we by sky notes, that the aesthetics of a well-conceived bottom note often go by underappreciated. As delectable as they may be, bottom notes are a rare thing on today's popular records. A bottom note is not your average (comfort-zone) low note, which should not pose a great deal of difficulty for a capable enough singer. Bottom notes are more challenging to sing, existing lower down the scale and will more than likely give the unschooled vocalist a harder singing time if their technique is not up to par.

Once you venture beyond your lower-middle tone, you will comfortably sing low until a certain point. Beyond that point is what I refer to as your **Bottom Zone**, and it is when the developing singer sets foot in their Bottom zone that they can experience singing problems.

Clarity is top of the list. You want to avoid 'muddy' notes. You are striving for Quality of Sound in every sense. See your bottom notes as having serious weight to them. With practice and correct vocal approach, you will extend the range of your

LESSON 8

voice by a few notes at the very least, if not much more. So you will experience some level of bottom zone success, depending on your talent. Bottom notes are not a performance necessity but a performance asset.

I want you to perceive bottom notes from an eye-level perspective, as notes sitting in wait directly in front of you as opposed to below you. Always be aware of your Chin Status when negotiating bottom notes. Some singers are prone to dropping their chin (dipping) when going for lower notes. Do not feel you have to adjust bodily or make a point of doing something, in particular, to make the note occur. Note that bottom notes, unlike sky notes, may require some level of throat participation. Try to lessen the impact of your throat though, as much as you perceivably can. As with the singing of sky notes, it is essential to have air inside your tummy when you create and produce your bottom notes. The air will assist and support your vocals, helping you to achieve Quality of Sound. You will also be easily able to envelop your bottom notes with breath if you so wish.

Encourage Centre Action: feeling your bottom notes as transmitting from your chest along with your tummy.

Remember, successful lower note singing has as much to do with attitude and mentality as it does with technique. Whenever you are operating at the bottom end of your voice, launch yourself into **Low Note Persona Mode**. You can also experiment with producing your bottom notes in a stylised voice. Such action can help you conceptualise lower notes on a different emotional level.

A simple way to sing bottom notes on your own terms is to up the key of your chosen song (opt to sing outside of your correct middle tone window) to accommodate your voice as much as possible when you dig deep. So your vocal starting point will be higher than usual. You will give the impression of hitting bottom notes but in reality, are hitting less challenging lower notes. So when you go lower, the listener takes it at face value. The lower notes they hear will not be as low as they may assume.

Never rule out ending your vocal performance on a low note. So the last line, or part of the last line you sing, can consist

HEADING FOR THE SKY AND DIGGING DEEP

solely of lower notes. Or the very last lyric you sing can be an obvious low note. It can add that touch of vocal magic if done well. Listen to Buddy Holly digging deep at the close of Peggy Sue. '**And I want you Peggy Sue**'. So Holly switches to a lower register on the final line of the song to magical effect.

Whether you make use of bottom notes in your performances or not, by exploring the lower range of your voice you will open the door to exciting musical possibilities. If you are looking to add a unique touch to a vocal line, a well-conceived bottom note may well be the way to go. It will not only surprise the listener but will show your vocal versatility in a fresh tonal light.

Case Study 9

Search iTunes for ***The Most Beautiful Girl In The World***
performed by **Prince**

The Most Beautiful Girl In The World makes for a fantastic case study, as it has everything on offer vocal-wise. Prince does it all: bottom, low, high, sky, and falsetto verging on whistle voice; even his talking voice is on display here. Prince sings this song in a consistent high-sounding tone until the moment he talks: 'And if the stars ever fell one by one from the sky'. After the talking part concludes, we get treated to some fantastic mahogany bottom notes. Some outstanding virtuoso falsetto gesticulations follow, a few of which he sings in his impact voice! Impact falsetto is something you rarely ever hear on a pop record.

Prince's voice covers the whole tonal spectrum. This ear-catching track should inspire you to investigate your singing voice on all tone levels.

LESSON 8

Case Study 10

Search iTunes for **Kind hearted woman blues**: *Take 1* performed by **Robert Johnson**

Recorded in 1936, *Kindhearted Woman Blues* was legendary bluesman Robert Johnson's first recorded song. The song contains Johnson's only ever recorded guitar solo. Some sublime musical things occur on this track, such as Johnson effortlessly playing rhythm and lead guitar simultaneously. But it's his artistic use of falsetto (often described as 'eerie') that elevates this track for me and adds to its mystique.

There has been much controversy as to whether or not we are hearing Johnson's songs at the correct tempo and pitch. Some believe his songs may have been accidentally or deliberately speeded up. I must say that I have played Johnson's songs at various slower speeds and although there's a case for Johnson's voice sounding more realistic, it's all a bit touch-and-go as far as I am concerned. So I am still of the persuasion that we are indeed hearing Johnson's songs at the correct speed. And regardless of speed, that supernatural falsetto on *Kindhearted Woman Blues* still mesmerises.

Legend has it that Johnson went to the Crossroads and sold his soul to the devil in exchange for guitar genius. With Robert Johnson, there is a blurred line between fact and fiction. A fact that makes his music even more alluring.

LESSON 9

THE IMPACT VOICE:
WAKING UP THE SLEEPING LION

EXPANDING YOUR VOCAL EDUCATION AND ADDING TO YOUR ARSENAL OF TECHNIQUES

> Brace yourself for impact. The finale is about to land!

Your Impact Voice is essentially your middle tone blown up or magnified; your middle tone's alter ego. It's the voice you keep on a leash that quietly burns in the background like a lit fuse on a stick of dynamite and then bang! You explosively reveal its raw power at the right emotional moment as you shift gears and steer the song in a new heartfelt direction. Here you are in overdrive, revving things up regarding volume, strength, power and solidity of tone. See yourself as being in Roar or Blast Mode.

The modern-day pop divas such as Whitney, Celine and Tina are all champions of the impact voice, utilising full-on, hard-edged intensity to tap into our emotional psyche. There are two sorts of impact voice usage, both designed to blow you away from an emotional standpoint.

The first approach is to announce the impact voice suddenly, with no pre-warning or build-up: Sudden Impact Voice.

The second approach is to give the listener brief flashes or hints of the impact voice throughout the song until finally letting rip on the finale. Here the singer will exercise Artistic Restraint, holding back their impact voice before finally letting it off its leash to cause a stir: Delayed Impact Voice.

Levelled singing, centre action, throat disengagement and the secret technique are fundamental to impact voice application. Feel your impact notes broadcast from the centre of your chest: centre action. Keep your chin stationary and in line with the uppermost of your chest: levelled singing. Take any throat input

LESSON 9

out of the equation: throat disengagement. Have air in your tummy while you are in impact mode: the secret technique.

Note you are not shouting when you are in impact mode but lifting, magnifying, projecting and resonating your voice in a controlled artistic manner as you communicate volume, strength and power. And because you will utilise throat disengagement, you will do so without putting undue stress on your voice. Taking your throat out of the equation is the trick to successful and productive impact voice.

To finish, let's hear from two impact voice specialists: Celine Dion and Whitney Houston.

Case Study 11

Search iTunes for ***My heart will go on*** performed by **Celine Dion**.

Celine begins on the fringe of her correct middle tone window, thoughtfully expressing each line with breathy delicacy and finesse. She is singing with her mind; being fully in the moment. She keeps her impact voice on a leash, leaving it to burn quietly in the background like a lit fuse on a stick of dynamite! Over three minutes in and not even a hint of a low or high voice! It's disciplined middle tone territory all the way. A lesson in artistic restraint and holding back, and it's her clever use of restraint that makes the finale so effective when it finally occurs. Celine's vocal end-game is to blow you away emotionally! As she unswervingly draws you in, the momentum has been quietly gathering, the fuse steadily burning, and then bang!: sudden impact voice. The middle tone's alter ego, namely the impact voice, announces itself out of nowhere; finally set free from its sturdy leash, and the song magically takes on an extra dimension. 'You're here; there's nothing I fear'. The lion is awake, the grand gesture is complete. Celine goes into overdrive, powering through in spellbinding roar or blast fashion until the song's conclusion.

THE IMPACT VOICE

Case Study 12

Search iTunes for *I have nothing* performed by **Whitney Houston**

Houston presents the first four lines we hear in a winning sugar-coated middle tone. She continues conversationally: 'I don't really need to look, very much further.' And then we get hit with an impact power note and a sustained one at that! 'Can't run from myself, there's nowhere to **hide**.' And this is where Houston is on another level vocally because she follows up this impact power note by attacking the next set of lines also in her impact voice. Beginning with '**don't make me close one more door**' until beautifully winding down with the line: 'If I don't have you'. Wow! Enthralling stuff. The Song re-cycles and that sugar-coated middle tone leads us back into the hands of her impressive impact voice. 'I never knew **love like I've known it with you**'. She shines forward until we arrive at the killer line: 'Can't run from myself, there's nowhere to **hide**'. The sustained 'hide' shakes up the threshold with its undeniable raw power. Here is stamina in a class of its own because she then goes into overdrive, upping the ante: 'Your love I'll remember **forever**'. That 'forever', to my ears, is one of the most fantastic sustained singing notes ever recorded. From there on in, she sings with majestic authority and never lets up, until finally thawing out on the sentimental 'If I don't have you'.

Whitney's vocal-dynamic powerhouse performance on *I Have Nothing* is one of the most enigmatic and thrilling on record to date. A classic example of Delayed Impact Voice. Ladies, go back to this singing masterpiece every so often to remind yourself of the standard you need to aspire to vocally. This record is an impact voice gold mine and like the Bible, it has everything.

LESSON 10

IT'S ALL IN THE PHRASING:

THE PHRASING COOPERATIVE:
THE VERNACULAR OF THE MODERN VOCALIST
THE THREE-DIMENSIONAL VOICE IN ACTION

EXPANDING YOUR VOCAL EDUCATION AND ADDING TO YOUR ARSENAL OF TECHNIQUES

> There is music in the pause and during the space that follows the pause

A simple artistic aim should lie at the heart of the modern vocalist mindset: to express vocal lines in refreshing entertaining ways: to pursue the Original.

Over the course of a song, therefore, the modern vocalist should look to satisfy this artistic aim to some meaningful degree. And it is here that we enter the realm of **Modern Vocalism**: the philosophy and practice of insisting upon something more; upon making every note count.

The singer who adheres to modern vocalism is an **Open-Minded Singer**. Their central reasoning is that every vocal line potentially has more to say or offer than we at first assume. The modern vocalist will be entirely receptive to the Alternative. I discuss the Alternative in lesson 11.

To bring about and achieve refreshing vocal line interpretation, the modern vocalist will seriously take into account **Sound-Play** and **Rhythm-Play**.

Sound-play revolves around using timbre, nuance and inflection to help you achieve refreshing, entertaining vocal lines. Rhythm-play revolves around using time and space to help you achieve the same end. And it is here that what I have termed the **Phrasing Cooperative** comes into effect: **Dynamic Line Approach**, **Lyric Sculpture** and **Active Pausing**. All three vocal actions work in tandem to spark your singing creativity and help you access the elusive Original. Understand that the connection which forms between the artist and the

IT'S ALL IN THE PHRASING

listener begins with the Phrasing Cooperative. Your particular way of musically expressing yourself is critical to how you impress upon and impact the listener. Your singing has to first attract the listener if they are to embrace your voice. You set the connection in motion through an appealing singing sound.

To help attract the listener through an appealing singing sound, the modern vocalist will always be chasing after a *Three-Dimensional* vocal sound. Whereby your vocal lines ooze with Characterful Expression, along with personality and vivid colour. These will be vocal lines rooted in an artistic awareness of Soundplay (timbre, nuance and inflection) and how these attributes of Soundplay can bring uniqueness to your vocal lines as a whole.

Dynamic Line Approach

The modern vocalist will bring about dynamic vocal lines by skilfully making use of musical mediums such tonal variation, breath, vibrato, juxtaposition, etc. along with various kinds of impromptu such as nonsense syllables, humming and ab-libbing. See yourself as painting or colouring your vocal lines with these mediums into which you will infuse personality, character and attitude to further help your artistic aim: to express vocal lines in refreshing entertaining ways. To pursue the Original. Singing should be an adventurous and imaginative undertaking. And remember that each line you sing has the potential to give the listener a glimpse into the mind of the man or woman behind the voice.

Lyric Sculpture

Lyric Sculpture refers to how you go about expressing yourself when you open your mouth to sing. How you elect to implement time and space and rhythm will be a major contributor to defining and personalising your vocal sound. There are infinite ways to sculpt your vocal lines, and your foremost job as a singer is to find the most appealing ones. The singer's primary concern is to wake the lyrics up: meaning to bring them to

LESSON 10

musical life. How we attempt to bring the lyrics to musical life, as in how we musically communicate our emotions and feelings along with our personality and character, is what helps to distinguish and set our vocals apart. Another way to bring substance, depth or added life to your vocal lines is to give particular lyrics that extra bit of emphasis or *shine:* **Vocal Highlighting**. So you pinpoint key lyrics to 'elevate' your vocal lines if needed.

Active Pausing

Active Pausing is where you pause for a cause: to generate a meaningful effect on the rhythm. So the pause is one that you consciously and deliberately engineer to help in the quest to bring about refreshing vocal lines. Through active pausing, the singer can rhythmically influence how the listener hears and appreciates their vocal lines.

Active pausing revolves around subtle manipulation of time and space. Awareness of Time and Space while you are singing is fundamental to singing creatively. Active pausing can also allow you to unfold and **present your vocal lines in stages**. Such action has the potential to afford greater control and precision over the vocal line in slower tempo settings. So you intentionally break up the line to get a better handle on the line's overall delivery.

Active pausing is an art form within itself. The modern vocalist will view the active pause as a valuable musical tool that can determine line formation and trajectory; helping to render vocal lines in rhythmically compelling ways. A perfectly timed pause or a pause in the right place at the right time can bring added substance to what would otherwise have been a standard vocal line. Remember, there is music in the pause and also during the space that follows the pause. You must be fully open to rhythm, and its numerous possibilities. You can perform on, slightly ahead of or slightly behind the beat, to present vocal lines in a fresh light.

The Active pause is dual-purpose. From a technique standpoint, the singer can use active pausing to take stock of

IT'S ALL IN THE PHRASING

the following set of notes they are getting ready to sing; adjusting their technique accordingly if need be to sing what follows. For example, you could use an active pause as an opportunity to consume air to your stomach.

Never achieve active pausing at the expense of musical sensibility.

Active pausing is a covert technique. The listener should feel the musical effect of the pause rather than hear or be aware of the pause. Unless you intend to make the pause obvious, perhaps for emotional or dramatic effect, for example.

Case Study 13

Search iTunes for **You are all I need to get by** performed by **Aretha Franklin**

Aretha announces herself 24 seconds into the song. The very first impromptu phrase she utters is musical heaven. 'Oh, oh-oh'. A church-rooted holler that gloriously sets the scene and which she repeats 11 seconds later for good measure. Who needs to sing actual words, eh? Aretha's ab-lib says it all. She then coolly gets the song off the mark: 'Like the sweet, **morning** dew'. The Active pause that follows the lyric 'sweet' is barely noticeable yet influences and affects the trajectory of the line. Notice how she sculpts the lyric 'morning', extending it to three syllables. Most singers here would have sung the lyric straight; not having the awareness or imagination to toy with the rhythm. Look out for such lyric sculpting opportunities when presenting your own vocal lines.

'And it was plain to see; you were my **destiny**'. Hear the fantastic way in which she sculpts the lyric 'destiny': sharp around the edges and packing a punch. She slightly falls behind the beat when singing 'And it was plain to see'; landing back on the beat in the nick of time to sing 'that you were my destiny'. The lyric 'that' is barely audible (she just about squeezes it in)

LESSON 10

but it's of no real consequence as our brain fills the lyric in for her, regardless. This is confident, risk-taking, rhythm-play.

'With my arms open wide, I threw away my pride'. And it sounds like she is doing just that: throwing away her pride, such is her vocal attitude. She follows up by setting a new soulful pace: 'I will go, where you lead, I'll be right there in your time of need'. After that, we get bang-on-the-groove heartfelt Soul, right through the chorus until she starts over with a new set of verses. Note the way she succinctly rounds off the lyrics; a stylistic trait evident throughout the entire performance. 'Stand by you like a tree, **and dare anybody that try and move me**'. This line chimes with pure Soul and is one of the most superb vocal line renderings ever captured on a studio recording. The artist and the subject become one. Aretha is role playing, or role singing as I like to put it. When she warningly sings 'And dare anybody that try and move me', you better believe her!

The queen of Soul continues performing in the same vein, mixing finely tuned emotion with soulful precision until the fade-out. Aretha's eclectic vocal presses all the right emotional buttons. It really doesn't get much better than this. The phrasing cooperative (dynamic line approach, lyric sculpture and active pausing) are in full energetic swing from start to finish on this one. Vocal magic!

Case Study 14

Search iTunes for ***That old feeling***
performed by **Brook Benton**

It's time to turn back the clock and listen to a master technician at work: Brook Benton.

Benton displays his vocal pedigree from the off. The first line he sings, is classily presented in stages. 'I saw you, last night, and got that old feeling'. His first active pause comes after he sings 'I saw you'. The second, after he sings 'last night'. He sustains the lyric 'old' remarkably: a stylistic trait that sets the pattern for what vocally happens thereafter.

IT'S ALL IN THE PHRASING

Keep your ear on the *1 2 1 2* brushed beat measure that sets the pace from start to finish. Notice how Benton sings with total freedom and mostly behind the beat. He sets up and unfurls his vocal lines in a delayed-like fashion, but totally in keeping with the probing strings and the overall movement of the song. This performance is a lesson in utilising and maximising space within the timeframe of a given bar length.

The musicality of Brook's rich mahogany voice takes its cue from the active pause. His lyric sculpture is always an enchanting affair, and this performance is no exception. Brook Benton has impeccable technique and outstanding phrasing. His is a voice that is in total control. Study his vocal art, and you learn much of value.

Case Study 15

Search iTunes for **Will you still love me tomorrow**
performed by **Amy Winehouse**
from her **Lioness**: **hidden treasures** album

Although Amy's voice harks back to and is reminiscent of the sixties, her vocal outlook is very much modern. Winehouse's desire to flirt with rhythm is apparent from the opening lines of this gem of a song: 'Tonight your mine completely', 'You give your love so sweetly'. Listen to her rhythmical treatment of the words 'completely' and 'sweetly'. No British pop singer quite rounds off a line like Amy. 'Tonight**,** the light**,** of love is in your eyes'. (The bold commas represent Amy's active pauses). Listen to how she presents this line in stages for a more far-reaching emotional effect. Again she expertly rounds off the line with her stylistic treatment of the lyric 'eyes'.

This recording contains one of the great impromptu moments in modern-day pop music. A magic musical occurrence, where we hear Winehouse show her vulnerable side, 'losing her voice'. It happens on the third line of the bridge on minute 2.25 of the song: 'But will my heart be broken'. As she sings 'broken' her falsetto coincidentally cracks. There is quite an emotional build-

LESSON 10

up to this line, offset by the preceding two lines, and I can only imagine that the lyrics must have struck a deep emotional chord with her.

This towering performance is a rhythm-play tour de force, representing a talented artist at the height of her vocal thinking and artistry. For me, this track ranks as one of the all-time best cover versions.

Thanks to **Dino Ayala** for putting me on to this recording and inspiring this case study.

LESSON 11

THE SEEKING MIND FRAME:
CHERRY-PICKING **THE ALTERNATIVE** AND GOING AFTER **THE ORIGINAL**

EXPANDING YOUR VOCAL EDUCATION

> Does this vocal line have more to offer?

When we open our mouths to sing, we inevitably do so with a set vocal pattern in mind. So our singing course of action —how we format and present our vocal lines—is pretty much predetermined from the get-go. So we will typically go with our very own **Familiarity Disposition**: presenting our voice in a way that not only appeals to and suits us on a personal level, but what we believe also appeals and suits popular taste. So without a second thought, we revert to our tried and tested means of vocal expression, our established way of treating a vocal line. We 'sing safe' and by-the-book and therefore our vocal lines will mostly be habitual, customary or routine in their conception. Risk-taking so to speak will rarely be a part of the singing equation, if at all. Entertaining **The Alternative** (another way of vocally seeing a line) will not figure on our artistic radar.

Now, in all fairness, you are probably doing a fine singing job regardless of the Alternative and are more than happy with your familiarity disposition as it stands, especially if you are a professional or seasoned singer whose voice has already passed the test of appeal. This lesson serves to make you aware of The Alternative, to make you question whether you are representing a vocal line in the best way possible; whether there was a chance of the Original having a say in things. Sometimes it's those little touches that can transform a line, giving the line added colour, depth and meaning. And we are not just talking about the use of dynamic line approach, lyric sculpture and

LESSON 11

active Pausing here to help you achieve this end. Manner of delivery, as in attitude, is all-important in singing. Remember, it's not what you sing, but the way you sing it. Ultimately, you have to truly mean the things you sing. It can't be half-hearted. This is why possessing an expressive voice is so important. There should be a high degree of expression in your voice as you sing: **Detailed Vocal Expressiveness**. Aim to deliver expressive vocals. So your vocal lines should carry and convey detailed vocal expressiveness throughout if appropriate.

As you know the central reasoning of the modern vocalist (he or she with the open singing mind) is that every vocal line potentially has more to say or offer than we at first vocally assume or think. The modern vocalist will insist upon something more; upon making every note count. The modern vocalist, therefore, will possess what I refer to as the **Seeking Mind Frame**.

Every song you sing will present opportunities to present vocal lines in refreshing ways. The Alternative lies in wait. It's up to you to seek what it may offer. Over time, you will develop an eye for lines that have 'more to say'. At the heart of your vocal art will be the all-important question: does this vocal line have more to offer? Some lines will not be as receptive to reshaping as others, but some will be, and it is here that you will look to be inventive.

Ultimately, the modern vocalist is just that: an inventive singing machine. He or she will obey the laws of vocal propriety but will do so with a seeking mind frame; being at the ready to entertain vocal lines that embody a refreshing interpretational perspective.

LESSON 12

COUNTING ON THE DIVINE:
LOOKING AT THE **SELF-HARMONY** FROM A MODERNISTIC STANDPOINT

EXPANDING YOUR VOCAL EDUCATION

> To self-harmonise, or not to self-harmonise? That is the question

The self-harmony first came to public attention in 1947 when the Patti Page (1927–2013, American) became the first singer to overdub her lead vocals on a commercial recording. She would do so on her first hit: a top 20 song called *Confess*.

When you self-harmonise you are improvising on a theme. Here the artist has further scope to expound upon the lead vocal's melody. Self-harmony improvisation can be a basic or advanced undertaking. The most basic kinds of self-harmony are the echo vocal and the shadow vocal. The echo vocal is where the singer simply repeats lines stated by the lead vocal, and the shadow vocal is more like a call and response.

The principal role of the self-harmony is to add weight to the lead vocal's story, and there are a host of ways, other than straight-up singing, to carry this task out. For example, you can use various kinds of impromptu such as nonsense Syllables, humming and ab-libbing. But in this lesson, we will look at a more intricate, modernistic use of the self-harmony: the **Vocal Mosaic**.

The Vocal Mosaic

A Vocal Mosaic is an assembly or series of impromptus (nonsense Syllables, humming and ab-libbing) that work as a collective to bring about a grand musical effect. I like to describe the vocal mosaic as a panoramic musical snapshot.

LESSON 12

Michael Jackson's outro vocals on his recording *Human Nature* show the vocal mosaic in splendid action. You can go ahead with case study 16 before reading further to give you a full understanding of what I will be discussing.

It is through the vocal mosaic that the central theme, as expressed by the lead vocal, can take on different melodic perspectives; becoming an open catalogue of expanded artistic insights. The best place to showcase a vocal mosaic is probably at the latter part of the song, as with Jackson's *Human Nature*.

When integrating a vocal mosaic into your song, your primary goal is to create a compelling cascade of forwarding vocal motion to affect the listener's senses. You can make use of the various impromptus, namely nonsense Syllables, humming and ab-libbing, to carry out your Vocal Mosaic. The lead vocal is an excellent starting point to inspire counter melodies, but your ideas can likewise feed off the backing music's principal themes. Go with where the inspiration leads you.

There are no hard and fast rules for vocal mosaic construction other than to account for the listener at all times. The aim is to invite and compel, not overload or confuse. You want the listener to understand your mosaic every step of the way, so clarity is a must, even when your ideas overlap or spill into one another. Everything must make total musical sense.

To go about constructing a vocal mosaic, you will need access to a computer-based recording studio. You will be multi-tracking inside of a DAW (Digital Audio Workstation). Set up a loop cycle covering the section of the song, you will improvise too. You'll be recording a set of improvised vocals with each loop cycle as you hear the song play in your headphones. Go for three to four rounds of recording (three or four tracks). As some of you who are familiar with loop cycle recording will know, whenever you record a fresh track, your DAW will automatically mute and store the track you just finished recording on.

You can establish a motif to bounce off if you like. For example, note how Jackson keeps repeating 'Why, why'; using this motif to springboard his vocal ideas. So you can record your motif as part of your song before setting up your loop. So you'll be always hearing the motif in your headphones as you record your additional vocal tracks. When you have finished your target amount of vocal takes, assign them to independent tracks to enable you to playback all the takes simultaneously. Listen out for ideas which complement one another or nicely blend or fuse. You are also keeping an ear out for flowing musical continuation. Mute and unmute accordingly. Keep what appeals to you and discard what does not until left with the best of the bunch. Much of what you recorded, you may see as being fit for your computer's trash bin only, but you may come across great little moments which may well make it on to the final product.

Counting on the Divine

When creating your vocal mosaic, keep in mind the following words:

My focus-antennas are up! My mind is open and ready to intercept any musical thoughts that travel my way. Consider yourself as being in **Reception Mode**. Let your improvisational side run amiss! Go with whatever musical thoughts pop into your head. Spontaneity and going with the flow is the name of the game here. Receive without hesitation as you translate your musical thoughts into animated sound. You may only capture a tiny fragment of an idea, but that little scrap may suggest and lead you to something bigger later on. Run with whatever form of impromptu presents itself: nonsense syllables, humming, or ab-libbing. The Phrasing Cooperative should be in full swing: dynamic line approach, lyric sculpture and active pausing. Entertain vocal juxtaposition. Melody is something we all have inside of us. Summon it, and it shall appear. You'll be counting on the divine to bless you worthy musical ideas out of thin air.

The Vocal Mosaic is an advanced representation of modernistic vocal thinking and expression: the 'pursuit of something more' taken a step further.

LESSON 12

Case study 16

Go to iTunes and listen to *Human nature* performed by **Michael Jackson**

Take in all that self-harmonising magic from minute 2:45 onwards. Note how Jackson makes use of different impromptus as he feeds off the accompanying Music and his 'why, why' motif. As the mosaic plays out, lines spill into each other, etc. but at no point does the mosaic disconnect you. It engages the ear, never overloading it. Jackson's splendidly constructed and balanced cascade of forwarding vocal motion exhibits the powerful effect a vocal mosaic can generate.

LESSON 13

THE VOCAL STRONGHOLD:
THE MAKING OF A CAST-IRON THROAT

EXPANDING YOUR VOCAL EDUCATION

| *If you sing with care, your voice will always be there*

See your voice box as an engine. Engines require oil to run smoothly, and you will keep your engine oiled and running smoothly through daily singing. Daily singing will be your way of keeping your engine well-tuned and regularly serviced.

Day by day, focused singing is a practical way of keeping your voice able and ready-to-go; of keeping your voice in tip-top shape. If your engine is inactive for too long, it will go cold; stalling on you when you attempt to start it up. You want a voice that can go the distance whenever required.

My advice for developing singers is to do a minimum of thirty minutes per day of organised voice training. So you will exercise your singing voice over a set period to develop its potential. Tending to your voice in such a disciplined, committed manner will afford your voice **SPDS**: Strength, Power, Durability and Stamina. Various voice improvement piano scales should make up your vocal workout. You are mostly looking to strengthen your singing voice and thicken your tone. In time, a **cast-iron throat** will be your reward, a voice that will not only be powerful but will operate for extended periods without 'gassing out' or breaking down on you. Extending the range of your voice should also be on your agenda. Note that singing karaoke for 30 minutes can also afford your voice SPDS. You can do this once a week for your workout. Be sure to choose songs that accommodate your voice key-wise. If you choose to sing karaoke with the original singer's voice present, you can gain enormous insight into the inner workings of their technique and

LESSON 13

also learn plenty about the art of singing. As I like to say: the best vocal coach is your favourite singer. Sometimes you can also do what I call a **Freedom Singing Session** to change things up a bit: 30 minutes of continuous a cappella, singing whatever you like, or whatever vocal thoughts pop into your head. Just go with the flow here. You can also record yourself as you do so. When you listen back, you might just hear something you sang that you can develop into a song. So you are more or less utilising the Counting On The Divine Method here, as outlined in the previous lesson. Shut the door and switch off from everything; being alone and at one with your voice as if in prayer. Sing without inhibition. Sing with freedom (without inhibition), fully projecting your voice. Connect with it as it explores itself. Utilise all ranges: low, middle and high. See yourself as vocally searching. Your voice is something you have to investigate on all levels. Tune into what your throat/voice box is getting up to while you Freedom sing. Implement throat disengagement where you feel or sense it is needed. Remember to keep your chin in check. Strive fore evenness of tone and consistent pacing of note outlay. You want to achieve oneness of mind, voice and art.

When you do a Freedom singing session, you are never just opening your mouth and going through the vocal motions. See yourself as having a sit-down with your singing voice, where you have honest *vocal conversations* with yourself. You are seeking to understand the makeup of your voice and form a deep connection with your vocal tone. *Feel* your vocal tone. Aim to develop a full-bodied vocal sound that communicates strength, and that captivates and absorbs the listener. Above all, seek to have control over your singing voice at all times. Successful singing is ultimately all about being in full control. When we sing, we are expressing a catalogue of minute controlled efforts.

When you are Freedom Singing utilise such things as Strength or Power Humming. So here you are going after maximum volume while keeping your lips sealed. You are relying on nothing other than your pure voice to produce your sound. *Feel* your voice as you internally output it. It is important to explore all ranges when you are Strength humming. Low,

THE VOCAL STRONGHOLD

middle and high. To get a deeper sense of how your throat operates on all levels when it only has itself to rely on as it ventures to produce an agreeable and intelligible sound that has weight and projects.

When delivering your vocals, sing with a continuous confident open *flow.* You are naturally streaming out your vocal lines without any hints of *hesitancy*. This will encourage a balanced and smooth sounding singing sound. That will have a togetherness of tone and colour. Output your sound with a flexible stress-free *loose* throat—with a *silky throat*. Meaning A throat/voice box that feels *well-oiled,* aiding and comfortable to sing with.

Finally, when you Freedom sing, have fun. Play with your voice. Go where your voice takes or leads you. Listen to how Sinatra plays with his voice (from minute 2:22.), following it where it takes him as Strangers In The Night concludes. This is a natural, inspired happening, where the artist feels the song and responds accordingly. And it's these bars of playtime that adds magic to Sinatra's performance and ultimately what makes this recording so memorable.

For your vocal workouts, you can practice along with pre-recorded scales. The Web will prove an invaluable resource for easily finding voice improvement piano scales that will be suitable for your needs. Beginners should choose scales simple in design and comfortable to sing alongside with. The trick is to find exercises that are manageable but also testing. After doing five minutes of your chosen warm-ups, you will divide your workout between low, middle and high voice exercises. Make use of both major and minor tone based scales to make you familiar with all the different singing keys on offer. After each workout, your voice will gain something, will collect another layer of conditioning, and as a result, your sound will steadily thicken and gather in substance.

Understand that building your singing voice is a brick-by-brick process. If you rush things, you will likely suffer setbacks. Vocal durability and stamina are things you work towards slowly, they don't come overnight. Remember, handle your voice with the utmost care. When doing your workout, be aware of your chin

LESSON 13

status and forever be in voice preservation mode. Have room-temperature water handy during your sessions. It's vital to rest your voice if it is feeling out of sorts. Never force the issue if you are experiencing any awkwardness or discomfort. End the workout and thoroughly rest your voice. You can get back on track the following day. You mustn't push your voice when it is giving you warning signs. Don't feel obligated to complete your 30 minutes if such occasions arise. Quit the workout and live to sing another day as I like to say.

A lot of singers churn out random vocals here and there throughout the day and will think by doing so they are adequately exercising their voice. But such fragmented vocal activity involves no dedicated regime. It will not do your voice any real favours regarding achieving SPDS. Randomly singing here and there is a non-demanding enterprise and will not test or challenge your voice sufficiently. Your Voice needs a sustained, ordered purposeful workout. It is via a regime that real conditioning takes place, and how you ultimately forge a resilient and dependable voice of steel. You want a singing voice that will stand up to the rigours of demanding live performance and studio recording sessions. Pro singers can adequately handle a 2-hour live set albeit with lots of small-talk and water sipping in between.

Once a day, dedicated singing will furnish your tone with body and roundness, taking you ever closer to the elusive Recording Voice. You are working towards a professional sound that has depth, substance and presence. Eventually, you will get to the stage where your workouts will act as maintenance; preserving your gains.

Respect your voice at all times. Always be in voice preservation mode, even when you are not singing. Avoid unnecessary overexertion or wear. For example, protectively conduct your speaking voice if you plan to spend hours on end chatting on the phone, for example.

My last advice to you here is to make time for your voice, even if you lead a busy life. Stand by your goal! Shut everything else out for 30 minutes a day to spend time with your voice. Voice time! Your vocal workouts should be something you look

THE VOCAL STRONGHOLD

forward to and enjoy. It should never become a chore or a hassle. And make it your duty to investigate your craft on all levels. Find out the meaning of singing terms such as Vocal Fry and Head Voice, for example. You get to know and learn about your voice by spending solid time with your voice. Neglect your voice, and your voice will neglect you.

LESSON 14

A QUESTION OF VOCAL IDENTITY:
KEEPING YOUR VOCAL IDENTITY INTACT

EXPANDING YOUR VOCAL EDUCATION

> Always be a first-rate version of yourself and not a second-rate version of someone else
>
> — Judy Garland

Influence is something no artist can run from. It's the singing voices we hold dear that help shape and form our own singing voices. Learn all you can from the singers you admire by all means, but the voice you end up with should be yours and yours only. Emulate don't copy. An original voice is a key requirement of singing success. Always remember the old adage: Art is that which disguises art. Strive to obtain the *untraceable* voice: meaning a voice whose influences cannot be so easily discerned or pointed out, if at all.

Frank Sinatra and Nat King Cole are immense influences on modern-day crooners such as Harry Connick Jr and Diana Krall, whose passion for the sound of a bygone era is such that they have patterned their vocal style after their crooning heroes. However, it's still Harry Connick Jr and Diana Krall that we hear when they open their mouth to sing. Here is where imitation so to speak gets the green light, gets validation. Harry and Diana have, on the face of it, become the character. So when they sing, it's authentic. And what we get is the 40s/50s crooning sound with an updated modern-day spin to it.

Metal singers, for example, all sing according to the Metal Vocal Template which defines the metal sound: raspy, guttural, screaming vocals, etc. to name some metal vocal trademarks. So their voices are in keeping with the style of music they represent. The best metal singers though shine through the template, regardless; finding their own sound and separating themselves from the pack (who are also implementing the same

A QUESTION OF VOCAL IDENTITY

Metal Vocal Template). So your chosen genre of music will have a large say in the way you sing, which makes striving for vocal originality even more essential if you wish to stand out from the crowd.

An original sounding voice is what you need to be going after. The moment you sing, the public should instantly know it's you who is singing. Your voice needs to have the **Recognisable Factor**.

A lot of developing singers fall into what I call the **Commercial Vocal Trap**. So they adopt the vocal style and mannerisms of a commercially proven singer to win listener approval and acceptance. A singer whose vocal styling is not their own has what I refer to as a **Reference Voice**.

So here the singer's voice is usually an inferior version of the voice it is referencing. Your vocals, therefore, say little about you as an individual or about your personality. If you copy how someone else delivers their vocal lines, then you are selling your vocal identity short. Be yourself when you sing. Your personality and character must be at the core of your vocal sound.

Black music heavily influenced Elvis, but you still hear a white man singing when you listen to an Elvis recording. Elvis absorbed much musically, but when he sang, you heard Elvis Presley. His character and personality were part and parcel of his vocal style. And this is one of the key reasons his music still appeals and connects. Elvis's voice gives you access to Elvis, the man. We can say the same about Sinatra and Marley and so many other notable singers. Over time, you will discover your vocal signature. For example, Michael Jackson's high-pitched 'He-he' ad-lib is his vocal signature. Your vocal signature is exclusive to you and helps make you instantly identifiable to the listener.

One key to achieving a unique, original vocal sound is to stay true to your natural talking voice. The way you sound when you sing should bear heavy semblance to the way you sound when you speak: the Vocal Merge (speaking voice and singing voice integration).

Listen to the likes of Sinatra, Hendrix, Lennon, Marley, Wonder and so on when they are being interviewed. Their talking voice

LESSON 14

sounds exactly like their singing voice. Some singers talk with an accent, yet you hear nothing of their accent when they are singing. So their singing voice bears no true relation to their speaking voice. A British singer, for example, should vocally promote their British accent regardless of the style of music they are singing in. Take the British R&B pop singer James Blake singing *There's A Limit To Your Love*. Blake is singing in an R&B style, an American music art form, but he keeps it British all the way, championing his roots. When he sings the line 'Like a waterfall in slow motion', the pronunciation of the word 'water' is quintessential British. So although he is adhering to the R&B Vocal Template, he sings without compromise, giving his English accent full reign rather than succumbing to an Americanised version of his singing voice. American hip–hop artists so profoundly influence some developing English rappers that they adopt a quasi-American accent when they rap. They forget their roots and fall into the commercial vocal trap.

The sound of your voice is the sound of who you are. Honour your roots when you part your lips to sing. Allow the true you to take centre stage.

Another key to achieving a unique original vocal sound is to allow your mannerisms (your particular way of speaking) to come to the fore. So just as the sound of your voice is specific to you, your mannerisms will also be specific to you. By letting your natural speaking voice lie at the heart of your vocal sound, you will allow your mannerisms to come to the fore.

Ultimately, if you want to make a vocal mark, and to stand out in a big way, begin by simply being yourself. Let your spoken voice freely trickle into your singing voice, and you will be well on your way to having a unique and refreshing vocal sound. A vocal sound exclusive to you!

LESSON 15

CAPTURING THE MAGIC:
KEEPING IT VOCALLY TOGETHER IN THE PRO RECORDING ENVIRONMENT

EXPANDING YOUR VOCAL EDUCATION AND ADDING TO YOUR ARSENAL OF TECHNIQUES

> The right frame of mind inspires the right frame of voice

You are now at a high-end recording studio standing inside of a vocal booth, readying yourself to track your lead vocal. In the backdrop, on the other side of the glass, you can see the engineer fiddling around. You know it won't be long before he presses the record button. Hiring a recording studio is never cheap, so you will look to get the most out of your booked session. To ensure you get your money's worth, you must enter the vocal booth with a **positive recording outlook**. The right attitude and frame of mind are all-important when you are about to make a record.

In the studio, vocal technique is everything. It's all too easy for your Foundation to go out the window once you enter recording mode. So just before you sing, you will raise your **Vocal Shield**: establish and assert your core technique disciplines.

VOICE PRESERVATION
SECRET TECHNIQUE
LEVELLED SINGING
FOCUS

Memorise the image of the shield as shown here on this page and see it in in your mind's eye as you prepare to record. Your vocal shield will not only support your singing but will help defend your voice box against vocal breakdowns. If you have to

LESSON 15

do lots of takes, you can trust your voice to hold up without incident.

Creating a model 'Levelled Singing Environment'

Before you track your vocals, you can arrange your microphone and pop stopper to accommodate levelled singing. Do as I describe if you wish to choose this option:

Adjust the height of the microphone so it suitably sits in line with your mouth. It must be just right. You neither want to be reaching or dipping to sing into the microphone. Now your pop stopper should be such that the midsection of the microphone's face aligns to and is visible through the midsection of the pop stoppers circle of nylon. So when you look through the pop stopper, see a mic that sits flush centre. As you are recording, you will sing from a **central vocal perspective**. Aim your vocals directly at the bullseye of the pop stopper's circle. See yourself as singing into the very heart of the microphone that sits on the other side of the mesh.

The sheer act of setting up your microphone in this manner launches you into **voice preservation recording mode**. You are consciously creating the conditions to help promote vocal longevity as you record. If you prefer to record seated, try to avoid slouching. Let your torso gear towards being upright and aligned, to further assist your breathing and support your vocal overall. So here your chest should be a little forward and your shoulders a little back.

Now, as well as keeping pops and plosives at bay, the trusted pop stopper makes for a great distance gauger between the singer's mouth and the microphone. Manipulate the pop stopper to sit precisely seven and a half inches away from the microphone's face. Use a physical ruler rather than guesswork here. If you prefer the distance to be a little closer or a little further, for whatever justifiable reason, then that's fine. The most important thing here is to establish a definitive working or recording distance.

CAPTURING THE MAGIC

Sing roughly one inch away from the established pop stopper and aim to maintain this **one-inch singing discipline** throughout the entirety of your vocal take. Your head and mouth should keep in line with the Central Discipline format, remaining stable throughout. Remember, if you move your head your mouth also moves, taking you off-centre.

Establishing a definitive recording distance, along with one-inch singing discipline, will encourage an even-sounding vocal take in terms of level and shade of sound. If you will be bodily active while you are recording, do so with **central discipline** in mind. For example, some artists use Gesticulation to aid their performance.

> **Gesticulation** — to make gestures while performing, as for emphasis, to aid the production and placement of emotion in your singing to inspire a great performance.

Song Visualisation works along similar lines to Gesticulation. Song Visualisation involves seeing the song unfolding before you. So it's as if your mind is beaming visuals and images on to an imaginary projector screen hanging before your eyes as you sing.

If you make use of gesticulation, go about things in a controlled, noise-free and monitored manner. Your head should remain relatively still and directed towards the centre of the pop stopper. Only your upper body, arms and hands should portray gesticulative movement, which you should carry out quietly. Be mindful of foot-tapping or handling the microphone stand while recording. These actions can be ruinous to an otherwise great take.

Once you have prepared your microphone, you can ask your engineer to secure you an eq sweet spot. This will involve placing the mic in different spots until pinpointing the ideal recording spot for you to sing in. Such action will help counter too dark or too bright vocals. You want to have a mutual sound colour. Remember, if you have to go back and do additional vocals, you can create a marker where the engineer stationed the microphone. Doing so will give you a good approximation of

LESSON 15

where you need to put the mic to re-create a similar eq zone if the mic gets disturbed or moved while you are away.

For the more technically minded singers out there who are self-recording vocals at home, I will share a few things here about my personal home recording chain set-up. Remember, such things are subjective. What is ideal for some may not be ideal for others.

I lightly use external valve compression in combination with a solid-state phantom-powered Microphone. I also use the low-cut filter, de-esser and noise gate options on my external valve preamplifier. When I am recording I like to see the mic signal dancing within the 0dBu to +3 output metering level, occasionally finger-tipping the red. It's okay if the signal touches the red sometimes, as I find this lends a bit of presence and warmth to the sound. As long as the recording itself sounds okay, with no hint of distortion or adverse effect, then don't worry about it. You can invest in a vocal booth shield if you are recording vocals at home, which you will set up around the immediate area of your microphone; thus helping to create a neutral sounding room-free recording environment.

The Singer at ease Environment

A singer should always feel at home in the recording studio. Here are some tips for creating your **singer at ease environment**:

☑ Always have a bottle of room temperature water handy. Water will help to keep your throat feeling moist and help counter against unwanted mouth noises that a quality microphone will pick up on. Sticky lips are a prime example here, which results from a lack of fluid during prolonged singing activity. You can moist your lips every so often with a quick swipe over with your tongue, if you have no water at hand.

☑ Invest in a decent pair of super comfortable quality headphones and bring them with you to the studio. The headphones at the studio may not be ideal for you in terms of comfort and wearability. Also, there is the bonus of not having to share something many others have used. Not every singer likes to have two ears covered while singing. If you fit into this category, set one earphone off-axis, resting it to the side of your ear. Using a pair of closed-back headphones with one-ear monitoring capability (swivel function) will be ideal here. Your headphones should always offer uncompromising comfort and sound quality.

☑ Some singers struggle to remember lyrics, which can be to the detriment of a great vocal take. You can solve this problem by having a lyric sheet set up in front of you on a music stand.

☑ Specific lighting may act as an inspirational mood setter. If the recording area has a dimmer switch, adjust the brightness to your taste.

☑ Most singers like to hear a bit of reverb in their headphones while tracking to get their voice going. Ask the engineer to insert reverb in the signal chain according to your liking. Note you will not be recording this reverb, only hearing it in your headphones. It's always best to record the vocals dry and add effects later so you have full mixing flexibility.

☑ Consider doing a microphone shootout if a range of mics is available to choose from in the studio. The most expensive mic, or the engineer's go-to mic, may not be the ideal choice for capturing the true colour or character of your voice. A condenser is the textbook recommendation for recording lead vocals. Still, an excellent dynamic mic could be a better choice for your voice on a particular song.

The Fear No Note Action Plan

A singer can quickly become undone in the vocal booth when faced with challenging notes, such as sky notes, for example. Such notes usually feature at the song's finale and need to hit home emotionally for the recording to carry serious commercial weight. The singer, therefore, needs to be at the top of their game. Stand up to challenging notes by arming yourself with my **Fear No Note Action Plan**, making life in the vocal booth an easier going singing affair.

LESSON 15

Hold your Level. The developing singer will sometimes unnecessarily raise the level of their voice when going for higher notes. The trick is to sing at the same level but move your mouth closer to the microphone; letting the microphone create the volume for you.

Maintain good body posture. Avoid slouching. Good body posture aids higher note production.

Levelled Singing. Be aware of your chin status. The classic mistake is to lift your chin when going for higher notes. Avoid this schoolboy error at all costs to promote vocal longevity.

Centre Action. As you deliver your vocals, seek to feel your chest playing a role in the sound-making process; backing up and standing behind your note production.

Fear No Note Mindset. Confidence is everything in the studio recording game. You must be doubt-free as you go for any challenging notes. Full belief in your technique allows you to sing with greater freedom.

Throat disengagement. Let the notes occur of their own accord, with minimal to no throat involvement.

The Secret Technique. Always have a good helping of air present in your belly while producing sky, bottom, falsetto or whistle notes.

Focus. Stay mentally connected every step of the sky and bottom note-making way.

Always listen to what your voice is telling you. Take some time out if your voice is feeling agitated. Always be in voice preservation mode, protecting your voice at all times as you sing.

Stay relaxed. Keeping your neck, throat and shoulders relaxed and tension-free aids going for challenging notes. You want to inspire relaxed and tension-free singing at all times, diffusing any stress or pressure build-up to your voice box while you are singing.

CAPTURING THE MAGIC

Studio Performance checklist

- ☆ Am I pleased with my performance overall, or could I have done better?
- ☆ Did I capture the magic: the way I imagined the lead vocal would sound?
- ☆ Is my pitching spot-on and are all my vocals in tune?
- ☆ Are all the lyrics I sang cleanly produced, intelligible? And have I comprehensively tailed off all my words?
- ☆ Is my performance releasable? As in, is it ready for the populace to hear?

The act of singing will always have an elusiveness about it. On one day you may capture the magic, and on another day it just won't be happening, no matter how many takes you do. Recording in the studio should ultimately be a fun experience: as you sing from your heart and soul, do so with an inward smile.

LESSON 16

REVOLUTION IN THE MIST:
THE COMING OF INSISTENCE
ART MANIFESTO

EXPANDING YOUR VOCAL EDUCATION

> I don't feel like I'm singing, I feel like I'm playing the horn
>
> — Billie Holiday

Tradition has a claim on all us artist folk. We are indebted to the past immensely whether or not we realise so. When we sing, we are largely acknowledging what has been and gone before us. If you are a soul singer, for example, your voice is continuing the heritage of soul greats like Otis Redding, Marvin Gaye, Al Green and Teddy Pendergrass, etc. Artists who helped shape the soul vocal template you now adhere to.

Tradition inevitably leads to change, and change ultimately morphs back into tradition. What was once fashionable and contemporary is destined to become unfashionable and non-contemporary, and the cycle continues. Hip hop is a prime example of a music genre that went through its fair share of trends and developmental changes and continues to do. Hip hop even has sub-genres! such as Trap and Gangsta rap to name but a few. Hip hop is also responsible for Trip Hop coming into being. Art, like life, will always be subject to change. Art *feeds* on change; and though it may not always be to everyone's taste, change is fundamental for art forms to subsist. The artist who advocates change must come to the table with a firm understanding of their art form's historical past. To step forward, one must first step backwards. Change would have left behind a trail of footprints, no doubt, to help you retrace its timeline. All you have to do is walk in them.

A closer inspection of vocal change shows it is mostly synonymous with developmental change, as in the development of a new technology (for example the microphone) or a new musical genre. New musical genres forge their own unique vocal styles. Think rock 'n' roll here or contemporary R&B or metal, etc. and how these genres came in tow with their distinct vocal templates.

The dawn of the microphone and electrical recording was the catalyst for a whole new vocal approach: the crooner was born. Singers were no longer required to have big forceful voices but could focus on a much softer, intimate sound instead. Bing Crosby and co. would use the new technology to their singing advantage; setting the lead vocal off down a new path. As the lead vocal spread its wings, the vocal canvas needed a splash of colour. That splash of colour would come in the form of 'personality'. Enter a genius called Louis Armstrong, who was arguably the first recorded singer to show the full possibilities of projecting a personality through a vocal. Armstrong would become the pivotal singer in pop history, influencing practically every singer in the popular music spectrum. Armstrong also revolutionised vocal line interpretation, using the Phrasing Cooperative (dynamic line approach, lyric sculpture and active pausing) in exciting and refreshing ways. The way artists would approach a song invariably changed forever. And then there would be Michael.

Michael Jackson is the quintessential modern vocalist. The father of modern vocalism. For me, his ascent to vocal modernity comes into being on his *Off The Wall* album. The multidimensional *She's Out Of My Life* represents a new chapter in popular song interpretation, laying out a new drawing board for vocal line rendition. Intensity (as a creative device) gets taken to dizzying new heights on this emotionally fuelled ballad: a stylistic enterprise that would peak on his follow-up album *Thriller*. Along with the Intensity, each vocal line gets a full-on emotional commitment. Here is the art of utility, of making every note count, of milking the emotion out of every note you sing. It's all about the finer details. Every syllable gets painstakingly accounted for; the Phrasing Cooperative getting pushed to the limit. And as with Armstrong, the ripple effect would be huge, continuing until this very pop day.

LESSON 16

Historically speaking, **Vocal Intensity** has always been present in the pop vocal arena but not as a style unto itself or school of thought, so to speak. Jackson's vocal approach no doubt stems from the concept of 'insisting upon something more', which is the foundation of modern vocalism. As with Armstrong's use of personality, Jackson's use of intensity represents Vocal Change that stands outside of technological or genre influence. Their particular brand of vocal change derives from the mindset, which sets the platform for the vocal art that follows: I think therefore I vocally am.

Throughout history, Thinking Movements, as I have termed them, have reared their heads in various art forms. For example, Romanticism in Literature, and Surrealism in Art. Thinking movements are essentially movements whereby the abundance of the works produced directly result from the philosophical thinking behind such movements. A strand of thinking so potent that it invariably manifests itself into the subscriber's art. The internal thought becomes the external action.

In this sense, I propose that Modern vocalism is a thinking movement. The vocalist who subscribes to Modern vocalism will create vocal art in line with their strand of philosophical thinking: to insist upon something more; upon making every note count with the aim of bringing about refreshing and entertaining vocal lines. And their end vocal product will directly result from their way of thinking.

The Modern Vocalist in action

The modern singing voice is comparable to a prism; distributing itself into a spectrum of expressive colours. The modern vocalist will see him or herself as being a living, breathing, thinking instrument. The modern vocalist is the vocalist who seeks, who insists on something more. You are going after inventive and refreshing vocal line renderings, and like the boxed drawings in a comic strip, each line tells its own little striking story. The modern vocalist endorses the concept of a New Voice for a New Song: every song you sing should present your singing voice in

REVOLUTION IN THE MIST

a fresh shade of light; should showcase another dimension of your vocal artistry. The modern vocalist will forever chase the *Three-Dimensional* vocal sound. Promoting vocal lines that ooze with Characterful Expression, along with personality and vivid colour. The Modern Vocalist will sing by the following declaration:

Our voice is the lamp that shines brightly amid the bland cliched mist. We open our mouths in homage to our vocal forefathers. The history of pop looms over our shoulder as we consult the microphone. Images of singing greats flicker along the cascade of a running monotone film reel at the back of our minds. Our voice does not stand still: we are forever in pursuit of the vocal truth as the software canvas captures our artistic musings.

Case Study 17

Search iTunes for **Heebie Jeebies**
performed by **Louis Armstrong and his Hot Five**

This revolutionary recording makes for a compelling case study choice when you consider it took place in 1926, close to a hundred years ago. *Heebie Jeebies* is one of Armstrong's earliest recorded vocal performances and marks the emergence of his characteristic style of scat singing. The landmark track is almost halfway through before Armstrong's vocals are on display. And we are in for a futuristic singing treat as the seminal singer joyfully toys with the words in tow with the rhythm and melody of the banjo. This ground-breaking, ahead-of-its-time vocal performance is an improvisational tour de force, and it's as fresh and startling today as it would have been in 1926. Legend has it that Armstrong invented scat singing after his music sheet fell to the ground when he was recording this track; and not knowing

LESSON 16

the lyrics, he improvised nonsense vocables instead. Oh, how I wish!

Check out *Cheek To Cheek* from the album *Ella and Louis* (1955) for more phrasing cooperative magic. Armstrong goes to town on this track as does Ella. Listen out for when Louis and Ella join forces, singing alongside side each other in alternative keys. It begins on minute 4:50. This is musicianship of the highest calibre. If there is such a place as jazz heaven then this is the kind of music I believe you would hear there. For good reason, *Ella and Louis* is my all-time favourite jazz vocal album.

THE ART OF SINGING WITHOUT SINGING:

DID THE GOLDEN AGE CROONERS HAVE AN EASIER VOCAL TIME OF IT?

AN EDUCATIONAL ESSAY BY SEBASTIAN MARTIN SELBY

> I think I'm much more a singer than I am a crooner
>
> — Frank Sinatra

If you wish to broaden your understanding and knowledge of the popular singing past, then invest your time in reading this essay. You can easily find all the mentioned songs on YouTube and I encourage you to listen to each and every one of them to fully grasp my teaching. I now invite you to go on a musical journey with me. We will go back in time to explore your microphoned vocal roots, so you can hear where your present-day pop voice is coming from.

Lately, whenever the epitaph *crooner* crops up, one recording artist from the distant past immediately springs to my mind; and it's not Frank Sinatra, and neither is it Bing Crosby, whose names are synonymous with the epitaph crooner. If I had not extensively examined the Crooner Question, the classic promotional stills of Sinatra and Crosby would doubtless have been the first things to enter my head: a suited Sinatra standing before a vintage microphone sporting his trademark fedora hat, and a decked-out Crosby with his trademark pipe hanging from his mouth.

So, if not Sinatra or Crosby, then who?

The mystery artist is the all but forgotten Russ Columbo. Take Frank Sinatra, for example: his musical stature continues to grow, to where it is fashionable for today's younger singers to adopt his image and imitate his vocal style. The passage of musical time has not been as generous to Columbo, who, for me, is the archetypal crooner. I say this because his voice more than any other embodies the true essence of the crooner sound.

Now, although the ideology of crooning continues to this day, the golden age crooning sound à la Columbo is a product of its time and will forever stay that way. I mean, if a modern-day male artist, for example, imitated Columbo's vocal sound to the letter, would he still sell?

Having said that, what I first noticed about Columbo's *antique* voice is that it still presses its fair share of contemporary buttons. And that's almost ninety years on, which speaks volumes when you consider the legions of singers from the same period, whose heavily dated voices remain trapped in the era in which they first emerged.

To have a deeper understanding of why the golden age crooning voice lost its dominance and became passé, we need to turn back the clock.

I imagined myself as opening a rediscovered time capsule as I pressed the Play icon on Columbo's first commercial release, *Prisoner of Love*, courtesy of YouTube. What met my ears was a voice frozen in time, that as it melted, displayed the crooner sound in all its emphatic detail. Columbo lived and died a crooner, being a mere 26 years old when he passed. He had no time to refine his vocal art further or grow as a pop artist, as Sinatra and Crosby would do. The young Sinatra listened to and admired Columbo's records, and this alone says an awful lot about Columbo's vocal impact in the early 1930s.

What makes Columbo the right crooner choice for this essay is that the nature of his voice and singing are not up for debate. There is no question mark next to his crooner tag. Analytically, his voice ticks all the crooner boxes. Interestingly enough, Columbo did not consider himself a crooner; disliking the epitaph. Come to think of it, were there any notable golden age crooners not opposed to being labelled as such? But Columbo is as much a crooner as Otis Redding is a soul singer, and although we cannot overlook whatever an artist has to say about their art, they should not have the last word by any means. From the outside looking in, the window is sometimes foggy, and so the artist doesn't always see their art in its true context.

THE ART OF SINGING WITHOUT SINGING

On the up-to-date side of things, Diana Krall, for me, pushes the *crooner* envelope perhaps more than any other self-styled crooner in the modern era. There is a genuine sense of a singer who is 'out for something more' regarding the enactment of a vocal line. Her 2005 rendition of *White Christmas* is a testimony to this vocal attitude. As she is singing, you can almost hear her thinking: let's see how far I can take this. What adds flavour to Krall's *crooning* is the rhythm factor. On *White Christmas* her jazzy side wants in on the action and so we hear her Vaughan-esque renderings ambitiously testing the 4 by 4 pop waters. To get at the rhythm, she approaches the song from a syllable-based standpoint, charismatically dissecting the lyrics with a Nat King Cole-like coolness. Her passion is ever present as she seeks to carve out something boldly refreshing. I wonder what Bing would have made of her version of his mega-selling song. The contrast in the old and the new is all too clear. Their interpretations are worlds apart, showing just how much singing times have changed and moved on.

So, what exactly do we mean when we refer to a singer as being a crooner? A Google search tells us thus:

> A singer, typically a male one, who sings sentimental songs in a soft, low voice.

But this description doesn't tell you the full story. There is not a definitive answer to this question unless you decide, like I did, to look at the act of crooning for what it actually is: which is another approach to, or way of vocalising. So it comes down to a matter of vocal approach. Are you going to implement your voice in the nonstandard way or the standard way? The nonstandard way involves the application of what I have termed the Set Voice, and the standard way involves the application of what I have termed the Raw Voice. I will explain both Voices in depth later.

I contend that we determine whether someone is a crooner based on their actual vocal approach, over anything else, such as song category or voice type, as Google suggests: 'sentimental' and 'soft, low voice'. And if we are to determine

ESSAY

whether someone is a crooner based on their vocal approach alone, then most of today's so-called *crooners* are not exactly so. Artists like Krall, Connick Jr. and Bublé, therefore, are as Google describes: singers who sing sentimental songs in a soft, low voice. They evoke the crooner sound, but they are not crooners in the traditional sense; the crooner label need not apply. But, for the sake of uniformity and keeping with the worldview, I will refer to Krall and Co. as *crooners* throughout this essay. Hence why you will see the epitaph *crooner* italicised when I am talking about an artist who I don't regard as being a crooner in the traditional sense. The epitaph *crooner*, is a loose one; bandied about irresponsibly for close to a century.

An equally important question is whether crooning is legitimate singing or a variant of singing (another form of vocalising) like scat or rapping, for example. I mean, why the label? Why the need to differentiate? Shouldn't just *singer* suffice? The need for such distinct terminology makes it clear there is more to the crooning sound than at first glance, and to help figure out what exactly is going on here, what we need is a distinction.

During the 1965 CBS-TV documentary, *Sinatra, An American Original*, the man himself, made a highly interesting statement that can help form the basis of a legitimate answer to a legitimate, though moot question. The Crooner Question: so what exactly do we mean when we refer to a singer as being a crooner? Here's what Sinatra said.

> I think I'm much more a singer than I am a crooner. In the days of Russ Columbo and Rudy Vallée, I think that they were rightly termed crooners because they had very small, soft voices. They were very good at it, but when Bing came along he was more of a singer, and I think through the years most of us have begun to execute more singing than we did crooning. Rather than being nasal, or making cow-like sounds of moos and those utterances, you know.

Whatever Frank has to say regarding the Crooner Question is of considerable importance because from 1939 to 1954 he was

THE ART OF SINGING WITHOUT SINGING

just that: a bona fide crooner. From 1954 to 1994 he was no longer a crooner but 'much more a singer'. Sinatra is the only example we have of an artist who underwent this *crooner to singer* transition. So, if there's anyone who can shed light on the Crooner Question, it should be Ol' blue eyes, right? Well, not so fast, there's a snag: Sinatra is among those notable golden age crooners opposed to the epitaph *crooner* as his statement evidently shows.

Sinatra's 1965 CBS statement ultimately creates more questions than it does answers, both hitting and missing the mark as you will see. But it sets the stage for this essay and in its own way helps to unravel the Crooner Question.

Sinatra says some intriguing things that give us food for thought, such as 'and I think through the years most of us have begun to execute more singing than we did crooning'. So here, Sinatra looks to be suggesting that crooning and singing are two distinctly different things. And what precisely is Sinatra implying when he says he and Bing were 'more singers' than crooners? Is he implying that crooners are not singers in the legitimate sense? Or is he merely referring to technical capability and musical soundness as his words appear to hint at.

> Rather than being nasal, or making cow-like sounds of moos and those utterances, you know.

What we will find is that everything Sinatra says makes sense and adds up when applied to Vallée, but doesn't make sense or tally up when applied to Columbo. It's the mention of the name Columbo that stops Sinatra's statement from being a cut and dry case regarding the Crooner Question. If Sinatra had left Columbo's name out of his statement, I would more than likely have accepted his words at face value and thought no more of it. But it's plain to hear that Vallée and Columbo are uniquely different vocalists, and that Sinatra Should not have put them in the same bracket. So let's start by zooming in on Sinatra's words along with the two artists, Vallée and Columbo, who Sinatra thought 'were rightly termed crooners'.

ESSAY

> In the days of Russ Columbo and Rudy Vallée, I think that they were rightly termed crooners because they had very small, soft voices.

Like the Google description of the epitaph *crooner*, this sentence offers us little in the way of answering the Crooner Question. Sinatra's observation here works for Vallée, but not for Columbo. Vallée, a 'very small, soft voice', I can willingly go along with, but Columbo, to my ears, has genuine size to his voice. Vallée's voice is thin in comparison. The way I see it, if you are going to describe Columbo's voice as very small and soft, then you would have to say the same of Crosby, who Sinatra tips his hat to in his 1965 statement; suggesting that Crosby's voice is the opposite to Columbo's in terms of size and texture. For me, there's nothing to separate Crosby and Columbo in the voice-size department. So Sinatra's 'very small, soft voice' categorisation regarding Columbo is highly questionable.

What Sinatra further says is also off target when applied to Columbo, but on target in terms of Vallée.

> They were very good at it, but when Bing came along he was more of a singer, and I think through the years most of us have begun to execute more singing than we did crooning.

When I hear a Vallée record, I am convinced without question, that Sinatra is saying that crooning and singing are two distinctly separate or different things. While listening to Vallée's vocals, I had to question if what I was hearing was genuine singing or something similar or close to singing? I should add that I gave Vallée as much singing leeway as possible; switching off my contemporary ears to hear him in the context of his times. But I kept coming back to the same conclusion: whatever Vallée is vocally getting up to, it's *not* legitimate singing. Now you may rightly beg to differ; I am merely telling you how I hear it. Listen, for example, to his 'monotone' overly casual performances on songs such as *Doin' the Raccoon* (1928) *Come*

THE ART OF SINGING WITHOUT SINGING

West, Little Girl, Come West (1928) and *I'm Just a Vagabond Lover* (1929). My first impression is that he is talking in a quasi-melodic way. It's not straight-up singing, but more a hybrid of talking *and* singing [I hesitate to write the word 'singing' here.] Musical Talking feels like the most appropriate description. So you musically talk your way through your vocal lines, capping them off with the odd sung note when the mood to do so strikes you. You could also describe Vallée as 'voicing the lyrics' as opposed to singing them.

Such an approach makes no real demands on the voice box because you are almost exclusively operating from a speaking-oriented premise. You are not imposing your voice to any appreciable degree. You stay comfortable at all times, outputting your vocals in a relaxed, laid-back, unforced casual manner. The style, lies in the manner of delivery over anything else.

What's strikes me about Vallée's vocals is their willingness to stick to the plan, the gist of which is to observe a linear movement, with no form of musical mischief in-between. The vocal's design goes in one direction only (like a piece of fabric with a single pattern) with no venturing down any side roads or alleys along the way. It's ultimately a one-way plan going down a one-way street. The exploitation of Time and Space is not a part of the menu. Any rhythmical possibilities do not get tested, and I get the impression Vallée doesn't have much interest in testing them either. Therefore, my modernistic sensibility struggles to see where the art lies in all of this. If there is art so to speak, to my eyes it is looking like the art of singing without singing!

Now let me throw in here that sometimes I found Vallée's one-way style to be just the ticket; where it works in a big way. His 1931 rendition of *As time goes by* is an example of this. And we hear Vallée show another, more musical side to his voice with the 1937 chart-topping song *Vieni Vieni*, which hints at the direction Vallée's voice could have gone in, but he never continued in this vein. The Rudy you hear singing on his first major release *Right out of Heaven* (1928) is the same Rudy you hear singing in 1939 when his recording career was winding down. Now, before accusing him of being a one-trick vocal pony, what Vallée brings to the table is Consistency of Sound. He did not have the strongest voice, but he used his limitations to forge his own vocal thing: a sound specific to him, Rudy Vallée. Vallee kept strictly in his lane, religiously sticking with *his* thing all the way, and I guess an obvious reason for his doing so was that he was using a vocal formula that had already passed the Test of Appeal, so why tweak any knobs? If you hit upon a successful vocal formula then, by all means, capitalise on it. It is not always in your best interest to go against your formula, which some singers make the mistake of doing primarily because of their need to be an artist. The problem for Vallée though, was that the talking-based style of crooning proved commercially unsustainable; quickly falling out of vogue as musical fashions changed.

Johnny Marvin and Whispering Jack Smith have a highly similar way of musically talking their way through songs in the guise of singing. You sometimes get a sustained note or two here and there, but that's as far as it goes singing-wise. Listen to *Cecilia* (1925), by Whispering Jack Smith, and *Breezin' Along with the Breeze* (1926), by Johnny Marvin. What you hear is a talking based vocal sound that only hints at singing, nothing more.

The Google definition of the word *croon* is:

> Hum or sing in a soft, low voice, especially in a sentimental manner.

The keyword here is 'sing', just as 'singer' is the keyword in the Google description of the epitaph *crooner*. But there doesn't appear to be much singing going on, if at all, when I hear the likes of Vallée, Marvin and Smith. All three vocalists follow in the footsteps of standout pioneering crooners like Cliff Edwards, Nick Lucas and Gene Austin whose vocals also have a Talking premise, though not as marked as Vallée, Marvin and Smith's. You can describe Edwards, Lucas and Austin's vocals as alternating between talking and singing. So they offer a visible mixture of both parties.

THE ART OF SINGING WITHOUT SINGING

The distinction between the Talking style and the Singing style is obvious when you compare any of these six artists to Crosby and Columbo, for example, who have far more going on from a singing standpoint. Crosby and Columbo will consign the Talking Aspect to a rear passenger seat, and it will be the Singing Aspect that takes over the vocal wheel in a big way. Yes, the aura of the talking sound (the conversational, laid-back manner of delivery) will still have a significant say in things, but it will be the investment in actual notes that will govern the vocal sound as opposed to singing some notes and speaking others. And it would be the Singing Crooner Template that would stand the test of time, existing to this day, not the Talking Crooner Template, which was already in demise as the 1940s approached, coinciding with the flagging recording career of Rudy Vallée. No modern-day *Crooner* sounds like Edwards, Lucas, Austin, Vallée, Marvin and Smith, who all represent the talking style of crooning to varying degrees. Modern-day *crooners* do, however, have an awful lot in common with Crosby and Columbo, who represent the singing style of crooning.

I should point out here that unlike Columbo, Crosby did not land on the world stage as a singing crooner. His vocal roots stem from the Talking Format which he puts to interesting use on his earliest recordings. Bing would steadily progress towards becoming a singing crooner, and it wasn't a long process: a few years at the most. And this is the reason I label him a singing crooner above all, because the Talking phase only takes up a tiny proportion of his extensive recording career. Listen to *Can't we be friends?* (1929) for a definitive example of Bing musically talking or voicing notes. There are examples aplenty from 1926 to 1930 of Bing in talking vocal action if you wish to hear more examples.

From a developmental singing standpoint, we get our first glimpse of Bing, the future singer, on *Ol' Man River* (1928). Things progress with *Little Pal* (1929) and his voice looks to be more melodious than ever before on *Waiting at the end of the Road* (1929). Things heat up with numbers such as *Without a Song* (1929) and *A Bundle of Old Love Letters* (1929) as the 20s draw to a close. On *It Must Be True* (1930) we hear sustained notes at work. Pay attention to his vocal from minute 02:59.

>It must be true,
>I am with you and you are **mine**, **all mine**

And this is one thing that set Crosby's crooning sound apart: how he would give certain notes more attention—sustaining them to varying degrees like how a pianist would use a foot pedal to affect certain notes, for example—as opposed to putting every note on equal tonal and musical footing. The standard practice at the time was more or less to visit each note fleetingly (keeping them 'perfectly in-line') rather than making a point of altering their shape (playing with their length).

The Singer Train gathers in momentum along the tracks with *The Little Things in Life* (1930) and quickly picks up serious speed in 1931, beginning with *I surrender dear*. Listen to the almost operatic note Bing confidently hits on minute 3:23.

>**Oh** to you my love, my life, my all

So with each charting single, you can say that Bing gets closer and closer to becoming a full singer, along with becoming more and more rhythmically proficient. But none of the titles I have mentioned truly say full singer; the Talking Aspect still noticeably looms. It is only when we get to *Out of Nowhere* that we hear Bing singing in the genuine sense, as in continuously sounding notes for long periods. Yes, the Talking aura still has a firm presence, but what Bing is fundamentally doing with his voice is *singing*.

What's clear then, is that there are two types of crooner: the Talking Crooner and the Singing Crooner. They share some similarities, such as the conversational tone of voice, for example, but what sets them apart is their tonal way of vocally expressing themselves. One musically talks and the other musically sings. Crosby and Columbo fall under the classification of Singing Crooners: they are continuously singing notes. Vallée,

THE ART OF SINGING WITHOUT SINGING

Marvin and Smith are straight-up Talkers. You can say that they continuously talk! Any singing, if you want to see it as such, plays an altogether negligible role in the vocal scheme of things, comprising the odd sustained note here and there, usually to round off the vocal line. You can credit Vallée, Marvin and Smith as making musical talking a style of vocalising unto itself, and if I have to classify Vallée, Marvin and Smith as crooners, which the weight of history tells me I do, then I will label them as Talking Crooners, *not* Singing crooners. Edwards, Lucas, Austin are *not* continuously singing notes, but then neither are they continuously talking; operating on middle ground. So they interweave between talking *and* singing. We will also classify them as Talking crooners, chiefly because the talking aspect outweighs the singing aspect to a noticeable degree.

I should add here that there are examples of where the mould gets broken, of which Cliff Edwards is a case in point. So the talking crooner transitions into the singing crooner on a select number. Listen, for example, to two heavily contrasting Cliff Edwards performances: *I can't get the one for me* (1924) and *It had to be you* (also 1924). On *I can't get the one for me*, he ably talks his way through the proceedings. But on *It had to be you*, Edwards enters the realm of end-to-end singing, adopting a charming high toned voice to do so. The switchover is impressive. It shows that Edwards was versatile to where he could morph into whatever type of crooner he wished, depending on what approach tickled his fancy the most or best served the song at hand. Crosby does the reverse on the symbolic number *Brother, Can You Spare a Dime?* So here the singing crooner crosses over to the talking side of the crooning road, or in Crosby's case (a former talker) revisits former times.

Now let's compare Crosby and Vallée's versions of *Brother, Can You Spare a Dime?*, both recorded in 1932, to weigh in on how the two contrasting artists present themselves vocally on the same song. Although both men are talking their way through the lyrics, what Crosby has going for him, is musicality along with versatility. There is an intrinsic awareness of rhythm at work as Crosby gives his vocal a push by injecting it with Active Movement. So he is pushing himself performance-wise;

ESSAY

showing his voice in an ulterior light rather than causally going through the motions, as does Vallée here. Bing will adopt a lower-than-usual tone of voice for this recording, a voice which verges on the operatic as the song winds down. Crosby therefore pulls out all the stops as the song nears its conclusion, whereas Vallée, in contrast, appears to want no part of rising to the occasion at all. The word 'subdued' comes to mind. Being overly casual can only take you so far, I guess.

So, regarding Vallée, Sinatra's words are on point.

> But when Bing came along he was more of a singer.

I will biasedly suggest that what Sinatra is really saying here is that Bing was more of a singer than a talker. Bing is producing legitimate notes whereas Vallée is hinting at notes. Frank's words though are likely referring to all-round musicality. So he is probably implying that Crosby's voice was more musical than Vallée's, that his sense of rhythm, choice of note and application of tone are superior? And if this is what he indeed *is* saying, I would have to side with him.

So okay, we can hear that Bing was more of a singer than Vallée, but was he more of a singer than his fellow baritone, Columbo?

Well, after casting my critical ear over Columbo's discography, I would have to say that this is far from being the case. Columbo is Crosby's equal on all vocal fronts, being every bit the singer Bing was; continuously singing notes in a musically pleasing and appealing way.

If we are to examine things on a deeper level regarding vocal styling, there is no doubt Crosby's singing style greatly influenced Columbo, but that influence did not underline Columbo's vocal sound as it would so many of Crosby's contemporaries. Columbo brings something altogether different to the crooning table. What Russ had over so many of his peers, including Bing, was a grander sense of reliving the moment as the lyrics poured forth from his mouth. If the crooning voice was subject to being laid-back or casual, those features only went so far concerning Columbo. There's an underlining quiet intensity

THE ART OF SINGING WITHOUT SINGING

to his delivery; a prevailing sense of This is really Happening, and it's Happening Right Now. He wasn't just casually going through the vocal motions as do so many other crooners of the period, but melodically re-enacting the experience. Columbo would make use of what I refer to as the Inner Voice: the singing voice that unabashedly lays it bare. One can only wonder how Columbo's voice might have panned out had he lived longer. The vocal art more often than not further refines itself, matures like a fine wine, as the artist increases in years. I imagine his voice would have ventured into jazzier waters. Listen to him sensuously toy with the rhythm from minute 1:57 onwards on his recording of Just Friends (1932). His sense of rhythm is more contained and less intricate than Crosby's; doing as much as it needs to, never venturing too far out and potentially becoming undone. Columbo avoids the deep end, keeping his explorations simple but meaningful. He makes music out of empty moments (the spots he consciously doesn't cover with notes) which show a telling understanding of the musical relationship between Time and Space.

Switching over to Crosby, while exploring his late 20s song catalogue and also the bulk of his 30s song catalogue, I heard a singer who willingly concerned himself with the intricacies of rhythm. Crosby's investigative voice often likes to 'zigzag' as opposed to following a straight line, and he mostly pulls this off. I can only imagine Crosby, who had an affinity with jazz, was exploring his vocal art as he recorded it, setting out to push the boundaries of particular lines as he brought them to life via the intercepting microphone.

Regarding rhythmical understanding Crosby was ahead of the crooning pack. I did not always agree with his take on rhythm, choice of note or use of ornamentation, I might add; my contemporary ears finding some of his vocal line renderings somewhat ostentatious; but such things are subjective. There is much about Crosby that sounds current, but also much that sounds dated. You have one take to shine and it's all too easy to overplay. As the adage says: less is sometimes more; hence some of these adventurous vocal lines, I feel, come across as a little too busy. There's a time and place to be experimental: a

ESSAY

jazz record rather than a pop record I guess would be more fitting for some of the lines in question. Columbo though, because of his less ambitious take on rhythm and ornamentation, rarely ever puts a foot wrong.

With the passage of time comes new critical outlooks; the art of the past will always have to fight to prove its worth as it inevitably becomes subject to scrutiny further down the line. We also have to remember though that we are talking about a time when you had one take to give it your best vocal shot. So coming across the odd below par or second-rate vocal line, now and again, should be of no surprise. There's bound to be inconsistencies creeping in when you are dealing with a prolific recording artist like Bing Crosby who has a colossal body of work behind him. Overall, I derived much pleasure from retracing Crosby's early vocal timeline and it is clear to hear why he is such a monumental figure in the history of popular music. All of today's vocalists are hugely indebted to him.

To sum up then: if you are going to label Columbo a crooner, then you have to say the same of Crosby; I see no room for debate here. Both men were singing crooners full stop. When Sinatra says Bing 'was more of a singer' you have to be careful not to take his words as meaning Crosby was not or never was a crooner. Crosby was a committed crooner from beginning to end and *Learn to Croon* (1933), more or less, hands Crosby's vocal status to you on a plate.

Now, in the last part of his statement, Sinatra appears to frown upon and associate crooners with 'being nasal' and making 'cow-like sounds of moos and those utterances.' Well, there is something to be said about Vallée regarding the question of nasality. Vallée has a nasal voice, there is no question about that. But that is of little artistic consequence if you are nasal-all-the-way, which Vallée is: meaning his nasality is consistent throughout. Being nasal one moment and not the next hints at a suspect technique, which would cause an attentive listener such as myself to raise an eyebrow. So Vallée gets a pass here. His nasality therefore comes with the territory, it's part of the vocal package. If the artist is fully aware of their voice being nasal and embrace it all the same, then it's not for

THE ART OF SINGING WITHOUT SINGING

us to pass musical judgement. You either like what you hear or you don't. And with Vallée, the vast majority of the public liked what they heard.

As for Columbo, the tonal body of his voice consistently comes across as open in nature (channelling directly from the mouth) as opposed to closed (channelling through or leaning towards the nose). Recordings like *Prisoner of Love* (1931) and *You call it Madness* (1932) are a testimony to Columbo's openness of tone. So Sinatra's nasal implication doesn't carry any weight regarding Columbo. I should point out that there are moments when you could mistake Russ's voice for sounding closed, especially when he lowers his voice. But this is mostly down to the reproduction quality of the studio recordings themselves, which do not do full justice to Russ's lower register. *Just Friends* (1932) is a prime example of this, where you could mishear Russ's voice as going from open to closed after he lowers his voice to sing the song's bridge which I have highlighted in bold.

> Just friends, lovers no more
> Just friends, not like before
> **To think of what we've been**
> **And not to kiss again**

If you raise the nasality question regarding Crosby, you find that his failproof baritone rarely ever lets its impervious guard down. His tone is consistently open-sounding. Yes, given his extensive recording output, you will probably come across the odd nasally line, typically as an emotional shift in gears takes place. Once again we have to remember the One Take Factor. So expect to encounter inconsistencies.

So then, although Frank got Russ wrong at every turn, he ironically turned out to be right! Russ *was* a crooner, it's just that Frank cited him as being so, for all the wrong reasons. Well to be fair, he did say 'I **think** they that were rightly termed crooners' rather than 'they were rightly termed crooners'.

What we can say at this juncture is that the attributes given by Sinatra for determining a crooner are best applied to the

ESSAY

talking crooner, and *not* the singing crooner. It's important therefore to differentiate which type of crooner we are referring to when we use the epitaph *crooner*: the talking kind or the singing kind? As in the singing crooner or the talking crooner. Putting Columbo and Vallée in the same bracket was an oversight on Sinatra's part.

Turning now to Sinatra, you've got to be wary of taking the opening words of his statement at face value.

> I think I'm much more a singer than I am a crooner.

We have to put Sinatra's 1966 self-reference into proper perspective. The year he made this comment is relevant because at this stage his crooner days are well behind him. Note that he says 'I **think** I'm much more a singer than I am a crooner' rather than the more self-assertive: I'm much more a singer than I am a crooner.

If Sinatra's words come across as a little inconclusive, a probable reason is that his voice is a voice of two acts, that you need to view through two separate windows: Early Sinatra and Late Sinatra. And with that said, let us focus our lens on the man himself: fondly referred to as The Voice.

Until you explore the Crooner Question from the ground up, it's all too easy to categorise Sinatra as being a crooner full stop; a catalogue of error rooted in generations of inattentive listening. Sinatra is a unique singing case; one of a kind, in fact, because he would later fully tap into the Raw side of his voice. Crosby did not make such a transition, and neither did Columbo nor any other notable crooner. Their vocal approach (using the Set voice as their way of vocalising) never altered, they were Set in their crooning ways until the dying end.

For me, Sinatra was a crooner from 1939 until roughly 1954, using the Set Voice. From there onwards he adopts the Raw Voice. He morphed, almost overnight, into a different brand of singer: the Raw singer; trading in the Set Voice for the Raw Voice. So let me expound on the Set Voice and the Raw Voice here and come back to Sinatra later on. And for good measure,

THE ART OF SINGING WITHOUT SINGING

we will also cover the pre-microphone era voice, the crooning style and the Crooner Beat.

At the core of the performing voice lies The Need. The vocal art must first appease the Need if the singing voice is to pay artistic dividends. Regarding the crooner, whose voice tailored to the microphone, the Need called out for Vocal Consistency: in particular, consistency of tonal presentation. The voice had its back against the wall so to speak, and a dependable sure-fire way of vocalising was its answer to holding its own in a time when the singer not only had to produce the vocal goods in one effort (there was no means of editing in those days) but had to keep in check with the supersensitive new technology, namely the microphone which captures every little detail, desirable or undesirable.

Crooning offers the subscriber Vocal Assurance: a proven way of forming notes effectively and comfortably; a standardised uniform approach to singing that puts the artist in the Singing Safety Zone regarding keeping their vocal sound consistent throughout while accounting for all their critical vocal needs, such as singing high or low and singing with serious power if called upon.

The vocal approach (the way you exerted your voice), therefore, was paramount. And what better than all-out self-engineered vocal consistency to increase the chance of a quality vocal take while also taming the supersensitive beast: namely the microphone. You can see the crooning sound as being a made-to-order pre-packaged vocal sound. Like a McDonald's meal, the buyer knows exactly what they'll be getting when they order it. And this is the key to unlocking the crooning sound overall. I mean, why that specific policy of sound and presentation of tone? What we are asking here is what makes the crooner sound the way they sound? It goes beyond singing songs in a soft, low voice, etc. made possible by the microphone. The answer boils down to a voice that you can purchase. A voice that comes already assembled; ready to use out of the box. We are talking about the Set Voice: vocal consistency at your service.

ESSAY

The Set Voice

When you sing with a Set Voice, you sing to a tonal specification. There are pluses and minuses to subscribing to the Set Voice. A big plus is that the Set Format affords the artist Vocal Assurance once they open their mouth to sing or go into live recording mode. The Set Voice will ensure the singer tonal consistency and a balanced Sound Design. By setting your voice, you adopt a vocal stance that goes some way to counteracting the inequalities inherent with singing in a Raw natural voice. But alas, at a price: your natural mirror image singing sound, which is the big minus. So you will not be using your singing voice in its purest form. You could say a superimposition has taken place: one voice placed over or in front of another voice. Holding a stick mask before your face makes for a good analogy: one face placed over or in front of another face. So you will utilise a staged singing voice. A voice you bring into effect via your speaking voice. So you are choosing to sing with an alternative voice as opposed to just implementing your natural voice from the off. I go as far as describing it as another instance of singing without singing!

Another minus is what I refer to as Technique Presence: meaning the technique remains unmasked. So you can hear the technique at work, playing its role in the vocal sound's production. You can describe the Set Sound as being a 'synthetic' sound.

The Set Voice is largely a voice that you put on. The act of putting on a voice imparts that you have done just that. So you sound like you are doing the very thing you are doing: which is putting on a voice. In the hands of the right crooner, the Putting On Effect is not so easily detected. Crosby is an excellent example in this regard: his vocal individualism, strength of voice and shining personality override the Putting On Effect and wins the *war of sound*. With less talented crooners you will find that the Putting On Effect significantly imposes on their vocal sound.

Singing with a Set voice, on the whole, is an easier vocal undertaking than singing with a Raw voice. Vocal mastery regarding the Raw voice is more involved as you have to

THE ART OF SINGING WITHOUT SINGING

develop and condition *your* voice instead of being able to access and install a ready-made voice.

To sing in a Set voice, you place your tone. Here the singer will lift or lower the pitch of their speaking voice as they launch their voice into Set Mode. You could readily say a manipulation of some kind has taken place. You can see the Set voice as an extension of your normal voice. So, once you Set your voice in place, you work your sound off your established tonal plane (your chosen pitch); operating exclusively within your tonal plane's framework.

The Set Voice can appear bigger than it actually in reality is, allowing the singer to create the illusion of serious power. This is chiefly because offloading power in the Set Format, as opposed to the Raw Format, is a less imposing vocal affair because you are not stressing upon your natural voice but operating outside of your natural voice. So the power you generate is 'simulated'. Yes, technique comes into play also, with throat disengagement for example, but it's the Outside Factor that makes it possible for you to present your voice in such a magnified, strong way.

It is through Crosby and Columbo that the Set Voice becomes a recording force. Why? Because the crooner would invest in the business of wholesale back-to-back notes, taking the crooning sound in a new tonal-based direction. The conversational, laid-back aspect would remain, but at the core of the crooning sound would be a voice that made a point of singing the lyrics as opposed to musically *saying* them; a voice more interested in getting to grips with the notes themselves, seeing where they might lead or take you; fully investing in them rather than casually airing them. In the hands of Crosby and Columbo, the crooning sound will become more emotionally driven. The back and forth 'talk one moment, sing the next' light-hearted vocal style that was all the rage, would figure no longer. The remodelled Crooner Template called out for the production of notes.

The Set Voice is a product of the pre-microphone era voice. And here we will look at the way entertainers got the vocal job done before microphones became the mainstay.

ESSAY

The Pre-microphone era Pop voice

Before the microphone ruled the recording land, singers would endorse, with little to no choice, a loud, energy-driven, belting vocal style. Think vaudeville and Broadway here and sentimental or comic singers like Al Jolson and Eddie Cantor. Pre-electrical popular recording artists like Henry Burr and Billy Murray also fit into this category of big-voiced 'muscular-sounding' singers.

When performing on stage, singers like Jolson and Cantor, not only had to compete with the orchestra but needed all in attendance to hear their voice clearly and fully. So getting their voice across to all sectors of the theatre was an important aspect of their vocal art. The Need for the pre-microphone era pop voice, therefore, was Vocal Projection. And it wasn't only on the stage that projection held sway. It also mattered when you were making a record in the studio. Vocalists like Burr and Murray would have to appease the sonic demands of the giant-sized flared metal horn, which was the early 20th century's recording answer to the tape machine. The sound recording process was far from being an exact science, but making your voice 'speak to the horn' was, by all historical accounts, the name of the game. And the way you spoke to the horn (how you kept the imposing mass of conical metal happy) was by projecting into it with a powerful, consistent tone of voice. It was either that or the horn, which could only capture a limited range of audio frequencies, would struggle to represent your vocal effort in the best light. The singer, therefore, had to be vocally savvy enough to make the horn work in their favour. Achieving the right sound balance was crucial. Finding the right standing-spot in combination with dead on voice placement paid dividends.

Acoustical recording was the norm until 1925 before the microphone, radio broadcasting, amplification and electrical recording became the way to go.

Conveying vocal mass (serious volume along with a full-bodied weighty tone) is one of the key objectives of the classical voice, and because of the need to get the voice across fully, the pre-microphone era popular voice had a strong bel canto element to

THE ART OF SINGING WITHOUT SINGING

its makeup: the Operatic glimmering beneath the surface of the pre-microphone era lake.

To convey vocal mass for lengthy periods, your technique mattered. The pre-microphone era voice, therefore, was as much about the technique as it was the singing. The technique was crucial to the vocal outcome. Voice Preservation lay at the heart of things. The Pre-microphone era singer would go about their singing protectively to ensure their voice box was fully functional at all times.

A feature of the pre-microphone era vocal sound is what I refer to as Sound Enforcement: outputting the voice in ways that cater to and promote projection. For example, a heavy sense of the dramatic encircled the pre-microphone era vocal sound, which helped the voice to cut through and have impact.

The coming of the microphone would turn singers on to the delicacies of nuance, inflection and tonal shading. The softer, lighter approach brought intimacy and tenderness to the singing table. The vocalist could now delicately caress the ear, could explore and present emotion in subtler ways. Sound Enforcement would no longer have to be a part of the vocal picture; brought into play sparingly, if at all. You no longer needed the Jolson-like gesticulations to make your voice happen: you let the microphone do the talking for you. With the aid of the microphone, the crooner would sing on their terms, calling the vocal shots rather than having to bow down to the cold vacuous flared metal horn.

The new electrical technology was not suitable for everyone, though. Old habits die hard. The Big Voice did not always see eye to eye with the picky transducer (the supersensitive beast) that stood or hung before it, whose critical ears were waiting to pounce on the slightest inconsistency or non-agreeable tone. Some failed to see that the microphone was an instrument, something you could use to your singing advantage, something you worked with, not against. And many also did not understand that what was vocally appropriate for the stage did not always go down well on a studio recording; that a stage performance and a commercial record were two separate entities. For example, take Charles Hart's dated 1927 rendition of *Are You*

ESSAY

Lonesome Tonight, where he rolls his R's for dear life. Some vocal things are best left on the stage, though to be fair to Hart, his R-rolling would not have stood out like a sore thumb in 1927.

We often associate the crooning phenomenon specifically with the microphone's arrival, but Edwards, Lucas, and Austin were active crooners before the electrical revolution took place in the music industry. All their earliest recordings are products of the acoustical age. The microphone showing up turned out to be a huge bonus, a gift from the music-loving gods rather than a stumbling block. So unlike some artists who had to get along with the microphone or else, with the likes of Edwards, Lucas, and Austin, there was no sink or swim scenario or downsides. If you compare Austin's acoustical and electrical releases, for example, there is no real discernible sound difference regarding the production his voice. Austin's delivery, looks to be the same as ever, with no trade-offs.

So Edwards, Lucas, and Austin were already on to a style of vocalising that had all the right elements to gel with the new sensitive technology shortly to arrive on their doorstep. It would prove a match made in heaven.

We should see the popular voice as a developing force, going from the Set Format to the Raw Format.

The Raw Voice

We can describe the Raw Voice as your true legitimate singing voice. The voice that is the mirror image of your natural talking voice. When you sing in your Raw voice you are presenting your singing voice in its purest form. No additional layering comes into play; all of your voice's natural sound characteristics get to filter through into your singing unchecked. You can see yourself as 'singing without cover', or 'singing naked'.

With the Set Voice, you hear the method at work (the method is constantly on display) because the method is largely responsible for the resulting sound. What the Raw Voice openly offers you is Technique Invisibility: the singing voice, and the

THE ART OF SINGING WITHOUT SINGING

technique behind the singing voice, on the surface at least, present themselves as one.

The singing process you can say is automatic regarding the Raw Voice as opposed to being pre-designed regarding the Set Voice.

Compare Diana Krall and Russ Columbo's versions of *You Call It Madness (but I call it Love)*. When you listen to Krall, with her nuance-based everyday sound, you can hear that she sings the way she speaks, that her singing voice is the mirror image of her speaking voice. She is singing without cover; everything about her singing voice sits in the Real Zone. She is not putting on a voice. She is vocally operating in the vocal realm of One Voice, as opposed to Two Voices. But can you say Columbo's voice imparts the same impression? His natural speaking voice is not so easily discernible, if at all. Columbo is operating in the vocal realm of Two Voices, meaning he is using his speaking voice to instigate and bring about an alternative singing voice.

Now, although both singers are following the same crooning guidelines, what makes Krall inevitably modern is her in-your-face naturalness. Krall is singing in the vein of Columbo, but giving a wholly modern account of the crooning sound: Google description crooning. And if you removed Columbo's voice from his hiss-ridden Lo-Fi 1931 record (which sports a typical old-fashioned musical arrangement) and replaced it with Krall's instead, Krall would still sound glaringly modern. It all boils down to her approach to, or way of vocalising: Russ is implementing the Set Voice, whereas Diana is implementing the Raw Voice.

Now, this comparison is not to take anything away from Columbo but to differentiate the Set Voice from the Raw Voice. You must listen to Columbo in the context of his time, of course. When Columbo was at the height of his artistic powers, so too was the Set Voice. In those days the Set Voice was a foregone conclusion if you were taking the crooner route as a singer: the Set Voice came with the crooning territory and was a part of the natural order of things, or so they thought! Natt King Cole would have something to say about that, as you will learn later.

ESSAY

What I ultimately want you to take from this Russ-Diana comparison, is that even if an artist sings under the crooner banner (and all the crooner attributes are present) it does not automatically mean you should label them a crooner. Look beyond the slow-moving beat, the soft low voice, the relaxed, conversational manner of delivery, etc. and home in on the physical nature of the singing itself. Is the singer implementing the Set Voice or Raw Voice? Base your answer on what you hear (Set or Raw) before you classify. A singer implementing a Set Voice equals crooner, and a singer implementing a Raw Voice equals popular vocalist who sings in the vein of a crooner. So they utilise the key crooner hallmarks (low soft voice, conversational tone, etc.) but they are *not* crooners in the traditional sense because the Set Voice is not a part of the vocal equation. To be a crooner in the traditional sense, therefore, the artist must output their vocal lines from a Set Voice premise, and thereby operate under a Set Format.

Modern-day self-styled crooners (those who invariably sing from a Raw Voice premise) are recasting the crooning tradition; presenting it in an adapted Raw way, as opposed to upholding it in its original (Set) form. So yes, they evoke the aura of the crooning past, but at the core of their art is the constitution of a Raw sounding singing voice. The overall vocal outlook, therefore, is markedly current, as is the musical setting. But in the shadows stand the likes of Austin, Vallee, Crosby, Columbo, Sinatra, Cole, etc.

The Talking school of crooners (Edwards, Lucas, Austin, Vallée, Marvin and Smith) has a claim of sorts to being the first popular vocalists to light a candle to the Raw Voice. As to the uninitiated ear, they can appear to be mirroring their natural speaking voice as they output their vocals. So they can give the impression of being Raw. But an impression is as far as it goes, because their vocal cues from a Set Voice premise, as opposed to a Raw one. I guess what we can say is that the Talking school of crooners inadvertently opened the gateway to the concept of a Raw singing voice. The claim for revolution is only valid if the effort is a deliberate and conscious one.

THE ART OF SINGING WITHOUT SINGING

What no one can deny is that the talking crooners helped pave the way for the singing crooners stylistically, who adopted their relaxed vocal manner and conversational tone of voice.

From a historical viewpoint, we can see Edwards, Lucas and Austin, etc. as laying down the foundation of the crooning art, as getting the ball rolling with a hybrid of talking and singing. Vallée, Marvin and Smith, etc. would heavily streamline the crooning art, making it more talking-orientated. Crosby and Columbo would rein the crooning art in, reshaping its tonal curves and edges by steering its sound towards the production of actual notes. Sinatra and Cole would sanctify the crooning art. Brook Benton would glorify and further sophisticate it, and Krall and Co. would revamp it. And all the while, Tony Bennett would keep the crooning art alive and well.

The Crooning singing Style

The crooning singing style comes with its own set of key stylistic trademarks. When you think of heavy metal singing, for example, screaming guttural vocals spring to mind. These are some of the certifying attributes that help define and distinguish the metal vocal sound and contribute to the Metal Vocal Template.

The key stylistic trademarks of the Crooner Template are the Relaxed Casual Vocal Manner, Conversational Tone of Voice, the Extended Note and Vibrato Coating: occasionally applied to the Extended note.

The crooner, as with the metal singer, is, to a large extent, vocally following a set of guidelines: the advantage being that you instantly afford yourself Vocal Consistency and Sound Organisation. Your vocal sound, therefore, is at once Consistent and Organised. You know where your voice stands style-wise and you clearly understand how to proceed vocally.

The Extended Note is the crooner's calling card, permeating the pop ballads of the 30s, 40s and the early 50s. The Extended Note is where you hear the vocalist linger on the note as opposed to phrasing it short. The crooner will usually call on the Extended Note when rounding off or putting the finishing touch

ESSAY

(an artistic stamp) on a vocal line. The crooner (with the exception, perhaps, of Brook Benton) will more often than not execute the Extended Note without ornamentation or embellishment. Vibrato coating is about as far as it goes. So you wouldn't hear the intricate note-play associated with a modern-day R&B singer, for example, when such a singer lingers on a note. The crooner will sometimes use the Extended Note as a bridging device, linking or merging one vocal line with the next. Brook Benton is an excellent example of a crooner who occasionally utilises the Extended Note in this way.

It was the singing crooners, standouts like Crosby, Columbo and the early Sinatra, who saw the potential of the Extended Note from a wholly musical standpoint. In their hands, the Extended Note becomes more than merely a stylistic tool. So rather than just crank out the Extended Note to (stylistically) see out a line (which was mostly how the talking crooners used the Extended note) the singing crooners would use the Extended Note to connect the lyrical dots, as a vessel to transfer emotion and feeling from one spot to the next.

The Extended Note was no longer assigned to a line-ending role, it could pop up anywhere along the way; in the middle or even at the start of a vocal line depending on the crooner's mood.

Because of its distinctive trademarks, the crooning sound is one a singer can quickly assume and put into practice. You have the blueprint laid out for you; all you have to do is vocally abide by it. Listen to Nat King Cole's first single release *That Ain't Right*, recorded in 1942. Do you hear anything of the crooner in this recording? What you hear is a blues singer subscribing to the Blues Vocal Template. But the blues singer gets put back in the Experimental Box, and out pops the *crooner* for the pop ballad recordings released not long after *That Ain't Right*. Cole then would effortlessly assume the voice of a *crooner* after having a vocal change of heart, I guess. Note I have italicised the epitaph 'crooner' here because, as I will discuss later, Cole sings from a Raw vocal premise. He is not a crooner in the traditional sense because he does not utilise the Set Voice. Cole, like Krall, sings in the vein of a crooner, embracing the key

THE ART OF SINGING WITHOUT SINGING

stylistic trademarks of the crooner template: relaxed, casual vocal manner, conversational tone of voice, the Extended Note and Vibrato coating.

Singing to a specification (endorsing a vocal template) is far less challenging than 'singing off your own back', with no set of guidelines included in the bargain. Yes, you still have to be a competent singer, but you are getting a big stylistic head start. Your vocal course of action (stylistically) gets mapped out in advance for you. Some developing singers, for example, find singing straight-up pop vocals far more testing than singing other genres of trademark-based popular music. Because with straight-up pop vocals, there is no definitive template to work from, hence no clear-cut trademarks to feed off; to show you the way. You are on your own vocally, but the upside is that originality is much more achievable. That's why there are so few noteworthy *crooners* around these days. It's because you are up against a template, in this case, the crooner template, where the trademarks play a heavy hand in the overall vocal sound. So because the crooner template is very much to the letter sound-wise, too many of today's *crooners* fall into the trap of sounding too similar to their crooner idols. The voice must outweigh the template, not the other way around!

So, having a vocal design in place is all very well, but you may be in for a hard time squeezing out vocal originality. Sometimes the quest for originality amounts to a long road ahead. Any singer who outshines a vocal template, therefore, deserves a big round of applause.

Listen to the very first commercial releases of Frank Sinatra, Dean Martin and Sammy Davis Jr. *From the Bottom of My Heart* 1939 (Sinatra), *Which Way Did My Heart Go?* 1946 (Martin) and *Dedicated to You* 1950 (Davis Jr). From a stylistic standpoint, not much at all separates the three men vocal-wise. They all sound glaringly similar. Why? Because all three men are adhering to the crooner template religiously. Another factor at work here is the Crosby Effect. All three men approach the love ballad typical of how an up-and-coming vocalist during those days would: in the style of Bing Crosby, whose vocal presentation represented a proven formula for singing

ESSAY

sentimental songs. The Crosby effect dominates Sinatra, Martin and Davis Jr's first recording steps. Hence, their vocal identities become lost.

Crosby single-handedly put the Singing Crooner on the map, so it's no surprise that singers who were just getting their feet wet would play it safe by imitating him. And if not Crosby directly, then via Frank Sinatra, who was still, prior to the crucial year 1954, under Crosby's vocal spell. The Crosby effect is so pronounced in these three singing debuts, that listening to Crosby's renditions of these songs instead (if he did versions of them, that is) perhaps makes more sense.

Sinatra, Martin and Davis Jr. would all find their unique voices. In a 1965 Life magazine article Sinatra would say:

> It occurred to me that maybe the world didn't need *another* Crosby. I decided to experiment a little and came up with something different.

Dean Martin, in particular, would quickly shrug off the Crosby effect. Martin's vocal art lay in distributing his vocal lines with contrasting degrees of vocal strength as opposed to catering to the implications of rhythm. With Martin, the rhythm was something you touched upon lightly rather than fully invest in or truly explore. His light-hearted sound and amicable tone would develop into one that accented the personality, as did Armstrong's. And like Armstrong, he carried that rare trait in his voice as he sang: the I'm Enjoying Myself Trait. You can hear it in his voice that he is having fun entertaining you. Dean gives the impression he is singing to a dear friend, and that dear friend is you. Martin would never truly let go of the Set Voice in the way Sinatra would. When listening to some of his later recordings, it's as if you hear his Raw side making a bid to take over. But the Set Voice comes out on top.

Sammy Davis Jr. never let go of the Set Voice either. Jr. looks as if he will make the Raw transition on his 1960 version of the Ray Charles number *I Got a Woman*. He hovers above the Raw; giving the impression he will land on Raw ground at any

THE ART OF SINGING WITHOUT SINGING

moment but never quite does so. Ultimately, as with Martin, the Set Voice has the last say.

Regarding influences though, no man is a vocal island; not even a crooning titan like Bing Crosby. All singing voices have to come from somewhere, and once you listen to Gene Austin (a hugely popular artist in his day), you can hear his obvious vocal influence on Crosby. Austin's softer sounding tenor vocals were in stark contrast to and a departure from old school belting tenors like Henry burr, for example. If we compare Burr's *Are You Lonesome Tonight* (1927) to Austin's *Blue Heaven* (also 1927), the contrast in vocal performances is like night and day. By today's standards, Burr's overdressed lumbering performance strikes me as uneven in its tonal presentation and overall construction. Never, at any point, does it settle down into something definably linear. My contemporary ears found his vocal thinking somewhat confusing, mostly because Burr appears to be in two vocal minds: the pop mind and the operatic mind. You can't have it both ways. Not on a pop record anyway.

Austin's whimsical performance, in contrast, is a different kettle of fish. His vocal offering is far more relaxed and lighter in texture: he is Singing at Ease. The emphasis is not so much on strength and power but overall mood and vibe. He's not looking to stamp his voice on the proceedings but lightly tip-toe across. What we are hearing is the art of willing containment, a packaged sound that fully knows its boundaries and is wise enough not to wander beyond them. We hear an early example of microphone-friendly risk-free vocalising at its talk-crooning best. Austin sounds like a singer who is in tune with the microphone in front of him: he has a 'microphone mentality'. Burr sounds like he is still performing in front of the flared horn, or better still, on the stage: he has a 'stage mentality'. Austin's performance on *Blue Heaven* is ultimately an example of successful Singing to Specification. Ninety years on, give or take, *Blue Heaven* still defies its age, having hardly dated, and is a treat on the ear.

Crosby himself acknowledged Austin as inventing the crooning sound. I read little into this claim as my research strongly suggests otherwise. Cliff Edwards and Nick Lucas are more likely

ESSAY

contenders. Cliff Edwards had a string of releases throughout 1924; the remarkable sounding *I Can't Get the One I Want*, being one of them. Nick Lucas recorded *My Best Girl* on November 1924 (released February 1925). It predates Austin's first solo recording, *Yearning*, recorded March 1925 (released May 1925) by three months. Edwards and Lucas both utilise the same soft, casual-sounding, light vocal approach that Austin made his own.

It's no wonder Austin made such a deep impression on Crosby's early voice. Austin's music was everywhere. Escaping his influence would have been next to impossible. By my estimation, it is only when we come to Bing's first no.1 song as a solo artist, *Out of Nowhere* (1931), that Bing becomes his own crooning man. It is on this song that his formulaic crooning sound truly gets off the mark.

Leading up to *Out of Nowhere*, Bing's crooning sound had been figuring itself out, calculating its exact formula. We can hear these calculations taking place on some of the songs I mentioned earlier when discussing Bing's progression from Talker to Singer: *It Must Be True* (1930), *The Little Things in Life* (1930) and *I surrender dear* (1931). All these songs are with Gus Arnheim and his orchestra, and it's the orchestra that leads the way, that is the commanding force. The design format of the big band song structure geared more towards highlighting the band than the singer. So on all three songs, it's a little while before we hear Crosby take part in the action. Back during the time these recordings took place, a big band number would typically start with a lengthy musical exposition (a super long introduction), which was usually a spirited light-hearted affair, and the singer would perform accordingly when their chance came to shine. You made the most of your minute in the spotlight, showcasing your vocal talent for all it was worth before handing the stage back over to the band. *It Must Be True* and *I surrender dear* are classic examples of the Band—Singer—Band—Singer big band song structure format. So band starts things off, playing for a long duration—singer gets in on the act and performs for roughly 1 minute—band returns in fine style, playing for another minute—singer reappears to see out the

THE ART OF SINGING WITHOUT SINGING

number. Any of Bing's early work with Paul Whiteman or Gus Arnheim can show this Band before Singer structure in action.

The band was the principal attraction, not the singer. You could go as far as saying the singer was secondary to the band. On some songs of the period the vocals would feel like a mere formality, entering early, saying its little piece, and never returning. The singer was more of an addition; one of many ingredients in the musical pot. What you were hearing was never solely about the voice but a collection of various things that *included* the voice, such as fleeting trumpet and flute solos, for example. It was under such musical circumstances that Crosby honed his skills: Crosby, you could say, was more or less a guest vocalist. But that would soon all turn around when the singer, in general, became the draw; as in the reason for larger crowds turning up to the venue. The big band arrangers would have to go back to the drawing board and rethink the structure. The format would undergo a drastic scaling down with the singer in mind. So no more long-winded expositions or instrument showboating before you got to hear the vocalist, who would now had the responsibility of carrying the tune from beginning to end. The entertainment factor rested firmly on the shoulders of the person standing in front of the microphone. And it would be in a similar Voice Rules All setting, (the 3-minute pop record setting) that Crosby, the romantic crooner, would thrive. Crosby now had a wider canvas on which to exercise his craft, affording him more opportunity to reel in whoever happened to be listening in at the time, and he would rise to the occasion with flying colours: undressing his vocal lines at a steady meaningful pace (as opposed to hurriedly) as he seduced the listener.

So up until the release of *Out of Nowhere*, you wouldn't be wrong in saying that Crosby's vocal job description was 1-minute band singer rather than 3-minute solo artist; being the case even when he was working outside of the big band setting and his recordings tell us as much.

Now, although *Out of Nowhere* (a chart topping song) was a big singing step forward, there were just a few artistic loose ends left to tie up. Once it dawns on Bing that the overall vocal conception should be as unpedantic and linear as the fathom

ESSAY

Crooner Beat that steadily dictates the tempo of the song, his ballad singing would settle into something altogether more strongly rounded and outlined; something that boils down to a pragmatic *approach* to lyrical presentation, whose primary concern is to be appealing to the ear. And this is what we get on *Just One More Chance*, his next chart topper. The dynamism now lay in the mode of delivery rather than any undue fun and games with the notes. The lyric becomes the focus with Crosby more than ever before. Columbo tapped into this artistic concept very early: putting the lyric first. Sinatra would also make the lyric his primary vocal concern. Even the little ornamentations and embellishments (or 'special effects' as I like to refer to them) that Bing was so fond of implementing get brushed to the curb. Keep your ear on the highlighted line-ending lyrics as you listen to Bing sing the opening verse of *Out of Nowhere.*

> You came to me from out of no**where**
> You took my heart and found it **free**
> Wonderful dreams, wonderful schemes from **nowhere**

His treatment of these notes is subtle. He dabs them with pure vibrato (non-breathy vibrato). So he gives these line-enders that little bit something extra, as was often his custom when capping a vocal line. Now listen to the reverse on *Just One More Chance*. Pay attention to the highlighted lyrics in the song's opening verse. Unlike the opening verse of *Out of Nowhere*, Bing leaves these line-enders completely untreated, with no hint of ornamentation or embellishment.

> Just one more **chance**
> To prove it's you alone I care **for**
> Each night I say a little prayer **for**
> Just one more **chance**

What you ultimately get on *Just One More Chance* from a performance standpoint, in contrast to *Out of Nowhere,* is a grander sense of order: each line is working according to an

THE ART OF SINGING WITHOUT SINGING

overall structure, a bigger picture, rather than doing its own little thing. A methodical formulaic approach is at work, and like spokes in a wheel, every line contributes to the whole. The vocal configuration revolves around sustaining an appealing catalogue of conversational sound, ordered and structured in its layout like the boxes of a newspaper's cartoon comic strip.

So the feeling-out process for Bing to find his exact crooning formula would be a relatively short one. And what sealed the crooning deal is that Bing's 'new' pragmatic approach (to lyrical presentation) fused perfectly with a vocal property few singing voices are able to translate: The Heart-warming Effect! The result will be a highly sophisticated romantic crooning sound.

Just One More Chance instinctively brings together all the pieces, and we hear vocals that are physically trying to establish contact with the listener; to put an arm around the waist of a lady or a hand on the shoulder of a man. The tone of voice is one that both soothes, caresses and comforts. Couple those three attributes with the Heart-warming Effect and the romantic crooning sound is in business. And what's more, there were no distractions, nothing to divert the listener's attention as the musical seduction took place. Any instrument showboating, therefore, would kill the erotic tension.

Most popular ballad song recordings, leading up to the 1930s, were too perky and action-packed for the romantic crooning sound à la Crosby to get along with profitably. Listen to the love songs of Gene Austin and similar artists from the period, for example. It was never wholly about the voice. There were always two or more stars of the show. *Blue Heaven* was as much about the chirping birds as it was about Austin's vocal. And on Austin's *Yearning (just for you)*, the Viola, Guitar and Ukulele vie for your attention as much as Austin's voice does. What Bing's romantic crooning sound needed above all was extra time and no interruptions. And he would get just that. On *Out of Nowhere* and *Just One More Chance*, the musical accompaniment gets consigned to a background role once the intro is over with. Here you're meant to feel the music, not hear it! The music plays second fiddle to the vocal; built around the voice as opposed to contesting or sharing the limelight with the voice. The voice is running the show, is centre-stage.

If Vallée talked the woman into bed, then Crosby sang them into bed; and if Mr Columbo learned one thing from Mr Crosby, it was that romance 'had a sound': a sound that you could access by caressing the lyrics; by 'making love to them'. Listen to Columbo on *Prisoner of Love* (1931). It's only his debut release, but he already has the romantic sound down to a T. That kind of in-depth vocal offering isn't just plucked out of thin air! The footprints lead you back to a pipe-toting blue-eyed crooner. Nat King Cole would take the romantic sound courtesy of Crosby and run with it!

The Crooner Beat

The crooning sound and the Crooner Beat go hand in hand; one cannot get by without the other. The crooner views the crooner beat as the slow-motion tempo that liberates, where the one-two brushed beat is at your vocal service. Here the vocalist, more than ever, gets to present their vocals on their terms, to control and dictate the pace. Under normal 4 by 4 tempo circumstances, the pace of the beat is not so laid back, but in this slow-motion setting, the singer has 'all the time in the world' to conduct his or her vocal business.

We can see the crooner as singing from an 'expanded perspective', where the vertical lines defining the boundaries of each bar offer enviable leeway, of which the Extended Note is a testimony to. In everyday 4 by 4 pop, the notes nearly always get succinctly phrased as opposed to Extended or drawn out. It is the crooner beat that makes the Extended Note so applicable.

The closest thing we have in our day and age to the crooner beat is the R&B slow jam, which offers the same level of vocal freedom. The crooner and the R&B singer share the same vocal attitude towards the beat: I have all the time in the world. I would go as far as saying that if the R&B slow jam genre has a lineage, it leads right back to the crooner beat. The crooner is the slow jam singer's distant relative. What inextricably links them is the age-old Extended Note, which they both use in their

THE ART OF SINGING WITHOUT SINGING

own unique way. The crooner will execute the Extended Note in a straight-forward fashion (sometimes doing so with vibrato coating) whereas the slow jam singer will Extend the note in a melodically intricate way, sometimes involving vocal gymnastics. The slow jam singer will oftentimes exhaust the note, milk it dry if need be to move the listener emotionally; to affect the senses. The crooner, in contrast, will be more conservative with the Extended Note, shying away from any undue complexity; preferring to keep things simple.

In my book, Crosby and Columbo are none other than the fathers of the slow jam genre. Today's slow jam singers are a by-product of the golden age singing crooner, albeit without the Set Voice. Just listen to Crosby's vocal rendering on line 4 of verse 1 from *Out of Nowhere*.

> Made every hour sweet as a flower to me

If a modern-day R&B singer sang this very line over a slow jam beat (in the same way and manner Bing does here), would you bat an eyelid? Take the 30s musical setting out of the equation and overlook the fact that you are hearing the ancient Bing Crosby, and focus solely on the musical nature of the line itself. See what I mean? (Incidentally, here is an example of a Crosby vocal line rendering that has stood the test of time.) It has barely aged.

Now let's pick up where we left off with Sinatra.

The Raw Sinatra emerges on his 1954 album *Songs for Young Lovers*, a vocal change that coincides with his switching labels from Colombia to Capitol. What we hear is a singer who has not only parted company with the Set Voice but also the crooning sound's chief stylistic trademark, namely the Extended Note, noticeable by its absence on the ballads that make up *Songs for Young Lovers*. If Sinatra *was* a crooner in 1954, it was in spirit only. Once again, we determine a crooner based on what we hear: Set or Raw. From 1954 onwards, Frank would sing from a Raw premise.

By relinquishing the Set Voice and its trusty sidekick, the Extended Note, Sinatra not only cuts ties with the very

ESSAY

foundation of the crooning sound but shakes off the Crosby Effect once and for all. If we once again rewind to 1939 and have another listen to Sinatra's vocals on his first commercial release, *From the Bottom of My Heart*, what you will hear is an all-out (Set Voice) crooner, with the influence of Bing Crosby (who Frank idolised) clear to hear. And the Crosby effect would have a big hand in Sinatra's vocal sound on his 1946 debut album, *The Voice of Frank Sinatra*. With each album leading up to 1954, the Crosby effect would become less and less. He would finally be free of it on *Songs for Young Lovers*.

Sinatra's transition from Set to Raw took 16 years to manifest and it would herald a lifetime artistic change rather than a one-time experiment. The switchover at once affords him a voice more open to suggestion, sounding more automatic than calculated. The vocal presentation, although compendious in its composition, is more probing; taking its cue from The Happening, the Real and the Now. Gone also are any special effects; even vibrato coating gets its marching orders. A clear, naked tone governs the proceedings. The dynamism occurs through the inflection, nuance and above all, attention to detail.

Sinatra's farewell to the Extended Note seems remarkable at first, until you recognise that his new mode of delivery doesn't require its presence. The Extended note could well disturb the design and the balance. Sinatra is telling you in no uncertain terms that he is now 'more of a singer than a crooner'.

If we fast forward to the year 1958 (four years on from *Songs for Young Lovers*) and listen to *One for My Baby* for example, you can hear that the jazz orientated mindset, which is all over *Songs for Young Lovers*, continues to be at work here on arguably Sinatra's greatest vocal recording. If you compare the 1947 version of *One for My Baby* to the 1958 offering, the stylistic shift is obvious. The phrasing on the 58 version continues with what he started on *Songs for Young Lovers*: concise in presentation and making a point of avoiding any tinsel. With the Raw Sinatra, special effects will have to earn the right to have a place on the vocal canvas. Sinatra doesn't sit on any of the notes, but shuts them down as soon as they make their point or serve their purpose. There's no style for style's

THE ART OF SINGING WITHOUT SINGING

sake here; the dynamic lies within the sincerity of it all; the gritty realism.

> So set 'em up Joe
> I got a little **story**
> I think you ought to know

In the 58 version, this verse is more direct and to the point. There is no hanging around like in the 47 version. The lyric 'story' lasts no longer than it has to, which is in contrast to the 47 version where Sinatra extends the same note. So on the 58 version, Sinatra continues to snub the Extended Note. The power of the delivery mostly lies in the economy of the output; the discipline of putting the lyric first over anything else. There is no room for any self-indulgence here. A fresh vocal outlook is now clearly at work here over the crooner beat. The Space Factor (how short or how long the gap between the singing of one line and the next) is playing a telling role in things like never before, decidedly contributing to how the vocals impact upon the listener. The Happening, the Real and the Now governs Sinatra's vocal art at this point in his career: interpreting life as it happens and unfolds before you. Each vocal line represents a snapshot of life itself.

This contrast in style between the early and the later Sinatra is a recurring pattern on all his later re-recordings of songs he performed before 1954. Compare his 1944 and 1962 versions of *The Very Thought of You*. There is no better way to chart a singer's growth than hearing them re-record the same song many years down the line.

There is a time-lapse of four years between *Songs for Young Lovers* and Sinatra's prior album *Swing and Dance with Frank Sinatra* (1950) and during Sinatra's recording hiatus, rock 'n' roll was making serious headway. Artists like Fats Domino recorded consistently throughout these four years, 1950–54, as did Bill Haley & His Comets. Listen to songs like *The Fat Man* (Fats Domino), and *Crazy Man, Crazy* (Bill Haley & His Comets). On a broader musical spectrum, Folkways Records and Stinson Records would release a plethora of Leadbelly memorial albums

ESSAY

between 1950–54 following Leadbelly's death in 1949. Ray Charles was very productive during the years 1952–1954, releasing a score of riveting albums. Sam Cooke was making waves on the Gospel front, having taken up leadership of The Soul Stirrers in 1950. Sister Rosetta Tharpe would release the seminal album *Blessed Assurance* in 1951. In the world of serious jazz, the year 1950 would see the release of Ella Fitzgerald's *Ella Sings Gershwin*. And last but not least, Sinatra's Capitol labelmate, Natt King Cole, recorded some of his best-known songs during the years of 1950–54: *Mona Lisa* (1950), *Unforgettable* (1951) and *Smile* (1954). [I will discuss Cole's significance during this period, as it relates to Sinatra, a little later.

You have to wonder if the melting pot of progressive music during this period tapped into Sinatra's artistic mindset. It's an intriguing notion; more so when you take into account that Sinatra later struck out against the radical rock 'n' roll, which was causing a tremendous stir. There are just some things that occur in the world of music that you can't help but notice or turn a blind eye to, no matter how much you want to: rock 'n' roll, like hip hop was one of those things you just can't ignore. Sinatra's reaction to it was scathing.

In a 1957 edition of the Los Angeles Mirror News, the paper quotes a passage from an article Sinatra wrote for French Magazine Western World.

> My only deep sorrow is the unrelenting insistence of recording and motion picture companies upon purveying the most brutal, ugly, degenerate, vicious form of expression it has been my displeasure to hear. Naturally, I refer to the bulk of rock 'n' roll.

Interestingly enough, many of the landmark rock 'n' roll anthems were soon to follow *Songs for Young Lovers*. A few months after the album's release came Bill Haley and His Comets *Rock Around the Clock*, the song that would later kick-start the rock 'n' roll craze, first issued in May 1954 as a B-side to *Thirteen Women (and Only One Man in Town)*. The young

THE ART OF SINGING WITHOUT SINGING

Elvis would release his debut single *That's All Right Mama*, in July 1954. And in the following year, 1955, songs like Little Richard's *Tutti Fruiti*, Fat's domino's *Ain't That a Shame*, Chuck Berry's Maybellene and Bill Haley & His Comets re-released *Rock Around the Clock*, would light up the charts. According to Wikipedia, 'It was not until 1955, when Rock Around the Clock was used under the opening credits of the film Blackboard Jungle, that the song truly took off.'

If ever anything would be a threat to the Set Voice way of musical life, it would be a drastic change of pace. The sound design of the Set Voice makes it such that it does not gel well with a much faster tempo. A faster tempo fully dictates the movement of the voice, and if the voice cannot keep up or follow the pace, then it gets left behind. The Set Voice is like a fish out of water when you remove it from its natural environment. It needs the right conditions to be successfully put into practice, therefore; it lacked flexibility.

Rock 'n' roll was an altogether different animal than the cosy, sentimental pop ballad that gave the crooner a free hand regarding Time and Space. With rock 'n' roll it was no longer about the listener being comfortable in their seat but being on the edge of their seat. The rock 'n' roll vocal sound was all about energy and liveliness as opposed to being relaxed and laid-back. The vocals were grainy and edgy rather than smooth and rounded. Holly's hiccups and Presley's tremble would entice the ear, denoting a fresh way of vocally seeing things. Representing a departure from the Old Way. A changing of the guard would take place: Raw replacing Set. The Set Voice would become a victim of its own singularity; too Set in its ways to jump on board with the new high octane format.

Understand though that rock 'n' roll was not the comet that wiped out the dinosaurs, but a fast-moving train that left the dinosaurs behind. rock 'n' roll sets the demise in motion more than anything else. The change in musical climate called out for a more versatile singing template, and the Set Voice would have to step down; ending up flying the flag of nostalgia rather than taking charge of or heading a new musical movement. And if it weren't rock 'n' roll it would have been something else. The

ESSAY

onset of musical change that the 60s would usher in is a testimony to this. The Raw transition would be inevitable because the popular voice would have to be flexible enough to take on any new genre that came its way. And it is with the 60s pop explosion, that the Set Voice would finally fall out of favour, leaving the Raw Voice to rule supreme. The stylistic shift à la Sinatra would also take hold: ornamentation would get kept to a bare minimum. Any special effects would have to justify their place in the scheme of things. The emotional connection would stem from the Raw integrity of the delivery (think the Beatles, Beach Boys and the Stones) rather than any fancy play on notes. You could say that the voice became businesslike in its outlay, getting to the point in the most fuss-free yet impactful way possible. The Extended Note had to give a valid reason for extending itself. Style, for style's sake, now had a question mark over its head, and because of this new stylistic attitude, the Extended Note would go into semi-exile; resurfacing once the Raw dust had settled. It would find a home in the Easy Listening category, being revived by the occasional crooner Brook Benton on his outstanding 1966 RCA Victor album *That Old Feeling*.

Benton's protean voice is at home across a wide spectrum of popular music genres: funk/soul, jazz, rhythm & blues, rock 'n' roll, folk and country. But it is when he opens his arms to the genre of pop and the classic commercial (crooner-prototype) ballad, when I feel we hear Benton's voice at its charming organic sophisticated best, where his voice comes thoroughly into its own.

We first hear Benton the romantic crooner on his 1960 album *Songs I Love To Sing* under the Mercury label, with *Moonlight In Vermont* being the standout crooner track. But it is six years later on the album *That Old Feeling* that we get the definitive Benton crooning sound, where he goes to town on the Crooner Template (particularly regarding the Extended Note) armed with soaring luscious strings. The masterful Benton would not only revitalise the Extended Note on this album but also illustrate the Set Voice in a creatively compelling light: a Set Voice in search of adventure.

THE ART OF SINGING WITHOUT SINGING

When I listen to Brook Benton, I hear a lush adventurous voice. Benton's singing beams with Artistic Panache, something he would have gleaned from fellow balladeer Nat King Cole. His diction and articulation is second to none, and concerning being vocally bold and daring, Benton has no crooner equal. What I find so enticing about Benton's voice is that its primary concern is Characterful Expression. The 'modernised' Set Voice courtesy of Benton is constantly reassessing the possibilities of where and when to apply characterful expression during a vocal line's presentation. Benton will occasionally take the Extended Note to the brink: Note Prolongation. Listen to Benton singing *That old feeling Feeling* (1966). His vocal performance showcases the Extended Note and Note Prolongation to great effect, along with his grand use of vibrato. Almost every line he sings gets magically capped off with a vibrato coating. Benton's phrasing ideology is much like Cole's, to where I would say there would be no Benton without Cole. But at the end of it all, Benton's sound is all his own. Listen to his magnificent recordings of classic songs like *Love is a Many Splendoured Thing* (1966) and *A Nightingale Sang in Berkeley Square* (1966) to hear exquisite Note Prolongation in action.

> I may be right, I may be wrong
> But I'm perfectly willing to **swear**

Note his treatment of the lyric 'swear' on his recording of *A Nightingale Sang in Berkeley Square*. Note how the extension bridges into the line that follows, helping to launch and propel it.

> That when you turned and smiled at me

What ultimately defines Benton's sound though, is what I like to refer to as *patient vocals*: the art of controlled delay; utilising degrees of *holding back* to affect the presentation of the line you are about to sing. Rhythm can take on a new meaning, have wider implications when the singer holds back. Such action is only truly viable over a very slow beat, of course. With Benton (perhaps more than any other crooner) delay is an artistic tool.

ESSAY

His performance on *Moon River* (1966) best shows this delayed approach to vocal line presentation. If Benton's vocal line presentation is unique, then it is mostly because of his use of controlled delay. Here again, Cole's influence is apparent, but rather than an occasional device, as with Cole, Benton makes delay the cornerstone of his crooning art.

But the rock 'n' roll vocal did not altogether leave the Set Voice and its accompanying crooning trademarks on the shelf. Interestingly, when rock 'n' roll giants like Elvis Presley and Buddy Holly wanted to express their softer romantic side, they would sometimes give you momentary glints of the Set Voice; as if flirting or toying with the idea of the Old way, but never fully going through with it. So the Set Voice never gains true access or settles in something concrete. Holly and Presley always stay on Raw Ground. Elvis was adept at this: dabbling with the *Set* but keeping it unequivocally Raw. Listen to the very last line of *Can't Help Falling in Love* (1960). He sings the highlighted notes in a Set voice while keeping the other notes decidedly Raw.

For I can't help falling in love with you

And Holly does similarly on the two occasions he sings the line 'With those who really care' from his ballad *True Love Ways* (1961). So he consciously evokes the Set Voice on a specific recurring line but keeps the rest of the performance firmly in the Raw Zone. And it's Holly's Rawness, his thorough tapping into his natural singing tone that makes his performance on *True Love Ways* aptly convey the shy-like tenderness that it does.

Now, you would think the Extended Note would struggle to slot smoothly into the rock 'n' roll Vocal Template, yet Buddy and Elvis welcome it on board; adopting the note Sinatra left behind. The rock 'n' roll singer utilises the Extended Note primarily for dramatic effect over anything else. So yes, the rock 'n' rollers welcome the Extended Note on board, but wholly on their terms. A little modification takes place: they Extend the note three-quarters of the way rather than fully. Note

THE ART OF SINGING WITHOUT SINGING

Prolongation would never come into play, for example; that would be going a step too far. In their hands, the Extended Note does not function as a bridging device either.

Listen to Presley's effective use of the Extended Note on *Can't Help Falling in Love* and Holly's also on *True Love Ways*. With their fleeting usage of the Set Voice and the Extended Note, Presley and Holly quietly tip their hats to the past. When Holly and Presley are in ballad mode, labelling them rock 'n' roll crooners would not be far-fetched at all. Before Buddy and Elvis, there was Bing and Frank, and no doubt the two singing crooners influenced the two revolutionary rockers. It is on the slower beat that the singer will reveal their hitherto hidden vocal make-up. Where we, the listener, get a telling look-in on their vocal roots.

Now, if there was one crooner trademark that stayed in business, it was the use of vibrato coating to express select notes. You can hear Holly and Presley utilise vibrato coating on their respective songs *True Love Ways* and *Can't Help Falling in Love*. Elvis would make the tremble—a variation of vibrato coating—his vocal signature. And for the origin of Elvis's tremble, look no further than Crosby. Bing Crosby was arguably one of the first crooners to implement vibrato coating in an emotionally fuelled way, not just for style's sake. With Elvis in mind, listen to Bing singing *Out of Nowhere*. Focus on Bing's use of vibrato coating. Sounds familiar? For me, Elvis the balladeer is a remodelled rock 'n' roll version of Crosby, the romantic singer. Not just with Elvis's use of vibrato coating, but in the way he sometimes presents and his vocal lines. Their phrasing ideologies share similar patterns.

Musical talking, the vocal way of Vallée, Marvin and Smith, would go on to thrive across the Rock 'n' Roll uptempo beat. But the fundamental difference between artists like Chuck Berry, Bill Haley, Eddie Cochran etc. and later Jimi Hendrix, compared to and Vallée, Marvin and Smith, is that persuasive rhythm would lie at the heart of and govern the vocal delivery; the uptempo setting altogether forcing the issue: you either sink or rhythmically swim on the faster beat. You 'can't stand still', as in sing without true movement. With Hendrix, Musical Talking

ESSAY

becomes a vocal category within itself, a wholly legitimate form of serving and expressing the lyrics.

Whether rock 'n' roll and co. had a hand in Sinatra's Raw transition is up for debate, but regardless, we can see Sinatra's sudden leap in a new direction as the crooner establishment adapting to a changing musical environment, as making a bid to reflect modern times. And I would say it's down to this adaption on Sinatra's part, why the crooner subculture largely exists till this very day: because the main man went Raw. So it's the Raw Sinatra, as in Sinatra 1954 onwards, that has made a mark on all of today's so-called *crooners*; not the Set Sinatra, pre-1954.

I should point out that Sinatra was not the first Raw singing crooner (that honour probably goes to Natt King Cole) but Sinatra was the first and only crooner to transition from the Set Voice to the Raw Voice. And it is this bold transition that Sinatra scholars need to take into account when analysing his music. Every other notable crooner from the distant past stuck with the Set Voice throughout the entirety of their careers (Bing Crosby is the prime example here) but not Sinatra. He gave up a vocal way of life almost overnight; ending a 16-year relationship with his trusted 'other voice'. And that's what makes his transition even more remarkable: the willingness to re-strategise and sing from a wholly new premise: a Raw premise. It was a courageous move on Sinatra's part, and one that would have a lasting effect.

Regarding Nat King Cole, I can only wonder what Sinatra made of his singing and whether Cole's Raw-based vocal sound impressed upon his artistic mindset to any relevant degree. It is in 1950 that Cole's voice comes into its own, where he fully matures as a romantic singing *crooner*. His mature sound gets up and running with *Mona Lisa* (1950). *Unforgettable* (1951) would follow. What would the vocal mind of Sinatra have been thinking as he listened to Cole's ultra-smooth (Raw) performances on these ear-catching classics? Could Cole have played a pivotal role in Sinatra's Raw transition, or should all the honours go to rock 'n' roll? Did Cole's voice open Sinatra's eyes to a Raw perspective along with all its inherent possibilities, perhaps? When I hear Natt's voice, I hear a singer who found

THE ART OF SINGING WITHOUT SINGING

the perfect vocal formula. When he finally put all the pieces of the jigsaw together in on *Mona Lisa*, Cole's voice must have been a eureka moment for many a ballad singer during the early 50s. If you ask me, I would say without a shadow of a doubt that Sinatra was one of these ballad singers: for whom hearing the crooning sound performed from a Raw standpoint must have been nothing short of a revelation.

If the Raw Sinatra has made a mark upon all of today's *crooners*, then you could equally say that the Mature Natt King Cole also had the same effect; and what we hear in recent times is a vocal continuation of the Raw Sinatra and the mature Cole, but with a modern outlook. It is the Raw Sinatra-mature Cole singing model that today's *crooners* emulate, whether or not they realise so. And with that said, it's time to take a closer look at one of the most recognisable voices in pop history: Natt King Cole, the conversational singer-at-ease extraordinaire. The Singing Paintbrush! as I like to refer to him. His is the art of disguising art, where clarity of tone and precision-elocution become a vocal force to be reckoned with. As with the later Sinatra, I use the epitaph 'crooner' figuratively with Cole, as Cole does not sing from a Set Voice premise. It's possible for a casual listener to mistake Cole's voice for being a Set one, largely because Cole is so heavily invested in the crooner template; but no, his voice is persuasively Raw in its overall tonality, design and consciousness. The vocals steadily stream from a Raw premise: his speaking voice outlines his vocal sound.

Cole is the only *crooner* I can think of from past times who did not start his recording campaign with the Set Voice in tow. When he crosses over to singing commercial pop ballads, Cole adopts the crooner sound without its core ingredient: the Set Voice. Cole, therefore, is singing without cover; his voice stands alone. He takes on the might of the Crooner Template on his terms, coolly brushing aside the Set Voice to present the crooner sound in a never-before-heard light: a Raw light. In Cole's case, singing Raw was a conscious artistic decision. It was no musical accident.

ESSAY

But Cole's greatness as a singer is not immediately apparent when listening to his early ventures. It is the mature Cole that stamps his mark on our consciousness, not the 'developing' Cole. As I mentioned earlier in this essay, Cole began his vocal life as a blues singer (*That Ain't Right*, 1942) before jumping ship and re-inventing himself as a *crooner*. So Cole did not announce himself on the world stage as a crooner but as a blues singer. This is not unusual by any means. Cole is among a list of influential crossover black artists who began their recording careers by singing the blues. Little Richard was a blues singer before he was a rock 'n' roll singer and the Jazz pop crooner Billy Eckstine, who I will discuss a little later, started out singing the blues before he switched to singing popular songs.

It is this blues beginning that is most likely responsible for Cole taking the Raw sound on board when he jumped ship; being already versed in singing from a Raw base. Again, Cole's decision to *croon* Raw is no musical accident, it is a conscious artistic decision.

I Realize Now (1944) is where we hear the makings of Cole's Raw *crooner* sound. Cole appears to be testing the waters here, ultimately failing to make a concrete crooning impression, on me, anyway. What's mostly missing is Vocal Balance. We get Extended Note overkill along with disproportionate special effects, I feel. Cole is finding his footing, no doubt. He is much slicker and more in the Romantic Crooner zone on his string of ballad releases two years later in 1946, where we find him to be wisely conservative with the Extended Note and more in tune with his special effects distribution. With *You Call It Madness* (1946), *I Love You for Sentimental Reasons* (1946) and *Christmas Song* (1946), Cole's Raw take on the crooning template is making serious headway. He kept (vocally) growing and growing and would blossom on Mona Lisa (1950), which signals the beginning of the Mature Cole so many people admire. *Unforgettable* (1951), *Smile* (1954), and *When I Fall in Love* (1956) would further cement his status as a crooning powerhouse; securing his reputation as one of the most celebrated and important balladeers of the 20th century.

THE ART OF SINGING WITHOUT SINGING

Cole would hit his musical pinnacle on the syrupy ballad *The Very Thought of you* (the 1958 rendition). *The Very Thought of you* is a masterpiece of elocution-precision underlined with spot-on artistic panache. No other crooner quite understands the delicate nature of vocal breath like Cole does, though Sinatra and Benton could have a thing or two to say about that. If we home in on Cole's use of the Extended Note from 1950 onwards, we find that his Extended notes are always delicately mannered and expertly measured. Cole's subtle and instinctive use of Characterful Expression is a recurring theme, something Benton would champion, as pointed out earlier. The slower the beat, the more sumptuous Cole's sound becomes.

The Very Thought of You is a masterclass of controlling Time and Space: the vocalist entirely at the helm. All the ingredients get thrown in the *crooner pot* for this one; the lyric interpretation is visionary and Cole's velvet tone is at its alluring, romantic best.

If you really want to understand Cole's vocal sound though and shed light on how it crashed through the Set barrier in such a meaningful way, then it's important to investigate the process of Timescale Vocal Evolution. It's not just about Cole making the crooning sound a Raw enterprise or venture, but also about the finer details. The Rawness is just one side of his *crooning* story, it's a number of things, such as Characterful Expression and elocution-precision, that ultimately make the voice sound the way it does.

With Cole, the process of timescale vocal evolution has various angles and if you're not fully tuned in, you might just miss 'em. For example, Cole recorded three versions of *The Christmas Song* throughout his career, in 46, 54, and 62 respectively. On the surface, Cole's three versions appear to show no true timescale vocal evolution to speak of. He sets forth down the same path on each occasion, sticking with the same safe singing key (C# major) and utilising the same phrasing ideology. The Saturday Evening Post in 1954 quoted him as saying:

ESSAY

My voice is nothing to be proud of. It runs maybe two octaves in range.

Range though isn't everything. Regardless, Cole fully understood the meaning of staying in one's (vocal) lane and exploiting that lane to maximum effect. Key-wise, Cole's singing would never venture too far out to sea, always staying in familiar waters. He picks a comfortable key and operates within a specific range or framework, an action typical of nearly all crooners, though Sinatra might have something to say about that. You will never really hear Cole hit a truly testing or very high note, for example. Occasionally he will get brave and stray a little beyond the eighth note of his chosen singing scale, invariably in a major key. Cole, in true crooner fashion, pitches from the centremost of his voice to pinpoint accuracy, making his high-note acquisition a more straightforward and easier going process. His high notes, therefore, are comfort zone high notes; nothing to cause him to break a sweat.

Now, when you compare the 46 version of *The Christmas Song* to the 54 version, the difference between the two recordings mostly boils down to artistic panache. One version has it (54 version) and the other not quite (46 version). On the 46 version, Cole just isn't active enough compared to the 54 version where the Singing Paintbrush earnestly looks to impart his vocal lines with vivid colour. [When I listen to Cole, I hear him as constructing a painting with vibrant glossy colours, hence the sobriquet The Singing Paintbrush]. His voice at once sounds more picturesque, richer, fuller-bodied and polished on the 54 version. Cole as we know was four years away from full vocal maturity, so it comes as no surprise that the 54 version is objectively superior. He was a good four years into his maturity at this stage.

> Jack Frost nipping at your **nose**
> To see if reindeer really know how to **fly**

Listen to how he changes the nature of his voice on the lyrics 'nose' and 'fly'—panache in motion. These are exquisite

THE ART OF SINGING WITHOUT SINGING

examples of Cole utilising characterful expression. Those same lyrics on the 46 version sound tame in comparison. It's no wonder Natt kept going back to this peach of a song. For my money, *The Christmas Song* is one of the most lyrically appropriate songs ever put to paper. Its conception is utterly outstanding. Great songs are songs you can *view*—you see the images they conjure up, play out before your very eyes. *The Christmas Song* is such a song, conjuring up images to superb effect.

Compare Cole's two versions of *Don't Blame Me* (1948 and 1958) for the same timescale evolution pattern (from a daring standpoint). You can find his 58 version on his hypnotic 1958 album *The Very Thought of You*.

> The thrill that I'm feeling
> **Don't blame me**

Cole sings both versions of *Don't Blame Me* in the key of B flat major. On the 58 version, he adventurously notches his voice up when singing the lyrics *Don't blame me*; operating at the end of the B flat major scale: G G and B flat. And by going for an unexpected choice of note, the line has more personality to it than on the 46 version, where he safely stays much closer to home when he sings the same part; operating at the start of the B flat major scale: C D B flat.

Cole was not the only crooner who released his first commercial recording in 1942. In the same year, the standout black jazz pop crooner Billy Eckstine would release *Stormy Monday Blues* with Earl Hines and his Orchestra. Eckstine's first single, like Coles, would also be a blues number! But that's where the similarities between the two eminent artists more or less end. Unlike Cole, Eckstine announces himself on the world stage as a crooner from day one. So what we hear on *Stormy Monday Blues* is a crooner singing the blues in a full-on Set voice, and it's not exactly a match made in heaven but a fine outing nonetheless. Not to take anything away from Eckstine, the formulaic nature and 'thicker' tonal body of the Set Voice does not do the blues full justice I feel; the Set Voice not being

ESSAY

flexible enough. A lighter blanket of sound works better overall for the blues. So Eckstine's singing, although pleasing in a blues setting, is for me, more effective and better suited to an Easy Listening setting—the home of the crooner beat. And we get just that on side A and B of Eckstine's 1947 double-sided single release featuring conductor Sonny Burke and his orchestra. *This is the Inside Story* (A-side) and *Just an Old Love of Mine* (B-side) show a master (Set-based) vocalist at work.

Eckstine's voice is the Set Voice par excellence. From a technical standpoint, Eckstine never puts a foot wrong on any of his records, well not to my knowledge, anyway. Tonally, he is rock-solid. He had a thick-creamed commanding tone that cut through the mix like no other crooning voice before or since. A recording engineer's dream vocalist! Eckstine was one of the few singing crooners who beat the crooner template at its own game. Like Crosby, Columbo and Sinatra, he emerged on the other side with an original sounding voice that is still rewarding to this day and highly relevant. Eckstine only has to sing a few opening notes, and you automatically know it's him who is singing. Eckstine possessed the enviable Recognisable Factor.

Eckstine was a Set Voice loyalist, flying the flag for the Method until the end. A big what-if, at least for me, is what if Eckstine had followed in the footsteps of Sinatra and made the Raw transition? It's ultimately a redundant question. The recorded voice he left with us is one of the greatest romantic voices ever captured on wax.

When I listen to Eckstine, I hear another crooner lurking in the shadows. I am talking about none other than our man, Russ Columbo. If you want to unravel Eckstine's enchanting vocal sound, look no further than Columbo, without whom we may not have had a Billy Eckstine. Do a side-by-side of their versions of *You Call It Madness (But I Call It Love)*. Columbo recorded his version in 1931, and Eckstine recorded his fourteen years later in 1945. Columbo's influence on Eckstine is clear to hear. Regarding tonal authority, Eckstine possibly gives us a glimpse into how Columbo's voice would have fared under better recording conditions had he lived longer—a fuller, more upfront colour-consistent sound, with a cleaner sounding low end.

THE ART OF SINGING WITHOUT SINGING

Now, to wrap up the Crooner question, we have some unfinished business to deal with regarding the enigmatic Mr Columbo. In the beginnings of this essay, I said words to the effect that Columbo, for me, is the archetypal crooner, because his voice, more than any other, embodies the true essence of the crooner sound. To lift the lid on Columbo's quintessential romantic crooning sound, we must first put his singing into its historical context. We already know that Columbo's recording voice is a consequence of technological progress—the introduction of the microphone to the recording process. The singing voice will form a partnership with the microphone to forge a new form of vocal artistry of which Columbo would champion. And what Columbo laid down on vinyl would help shape the voices of two of the greatest singers of the 20th century: Francis Albert Sinatra and William Clarence Eckstine.

Sinatra and Columbo were both vocalists of Italian-American heritage like so many other notable crooners—Dean Martin, Louis Prima, Vic Damone, Jerry Vale and Perry Como being among them. As youngsters, both Sinatra and Columbo would have grown up to the sounds of Italian opera. The correlation between crooning and Bel canto singing is unmistakable, as is the Italian-American heritage connection. If the Extended Note has an origin, look no further than Bel canto singing. Here is what Sinatra had to say about Bel canto singing.

> What I finally hit on was more the *bel canto* Italian school of singing, without making a point of it. That meant I had to stay in better shape because I had to *sing* more. It was more difficult than Crosby's style, much more difficult.

These words are the continuation of the aforementioned.

> It occurred to me that maybe the world didn't need *another* Crosby. I decided to experiment a little and came up with something different.

And yes, you get moments in his singing when Sinatra hints at the operatic—the Bel canto Factor peeping through the crack in

ESSAY

the Easy Listening curtains. We can say the same for Columbo and also for Crosby, contrary to what Frank says regarding Crosby's style. There are many Bel canto references in the vocal work of Crosby and Columbo. According to Google, Bel canto translates to 'beautiful singing'.

It's well documented that Columbo was a capable opera singer. 'He (Columbo) had studied a little with Alex Bevani, Los Angeles opera star', according to the November 1, 1931 edition of Milwaukee Journal Journal in their article about the rising star Columbo. What's immediately intriguing about Columbo then, is here we have a singer who looks as if he could have taken either route—the pop route or the classical route. But he opts to go down a softer singing pathway, hand in hand with an adoring microphone. So Columbo adopted the crooning sound just as Natt King Cole would do. It's just that Cole tweaked the formula by singing from a Raw premise. Like Natt, Russ was talented enough to shine through the iron-willed Crooner Template and say something refreshingly new. The November 1, 1931 edition of Milwaukee Journal, also said the following of Columbo.

> He's not a crooner, a blues singer nor a 'straight' baritone. Instead, he has a technic all his own, a sly delivery of tone that weaves its way through a song in a manner hard to describe.

Could the 'sly delivery of tone' be referring to an art form that amounts to singing within singing?

Whether the golden age crooners saw their vocal art as singing without singing is something I guess we will never know, because all these fascinating singers, unfortunately, are no longer with us. I certainly see their vocal art in this unique way. So if someone asked me the Crooner Question: so what exactly do we mean when we refer to a singer as being a crooner? My answer would be—a singer who sings without singing.

Highly cryptic, I know, and I would follow up by suggesting they read this essay which would put them in the picture.

The last part of Franks Bel canto statement from the 1965 Life magazine article screams out at me at this point.

THE ART OF SINGING WITHOUT SINGING

That meant I had to stay in better shape because I had to sing more. It was more difficult than Crosby's style, much more difficult.

You can read a lot into these words regarding the 'singing without singing' supposition. Once again Frank appears to be saying that crooners are not singers in the genuine sense; that what he, Sinatra, is technically doing, differs from what he, Crosby, is technically doing. He said these words on April 23, 1965, and they strike me as somewhat inconsistent when you consider what he says seven months later (on the 16th of November 1965) in the documentary, *Sinatra, An American Original,* where he appears to be suggesting that he and Crosby are off the same vocal ilk; being more singers than crooners.

By distancing himself from the crooner tag, Sinatra is brushing aside the very thing that contributed to him becoming the phenomenal artist we all love. The truth of the matter is the Sinatra we hear pre-1954 is every inch a crooner regardless of whether he wants to acknowledge this. It all lies in the vocal sound's premise: Set or Raw. And what you hear from Sinatra prior to 1954 is undoubtedly a Set-based singing voice. It is only after he undergoes the crooner to singer conversion in 1954 that what we hear on his records, thereafter, is a Raw-based singing voice.

In retrospect, the story of the Popular vocal truly begins with the golden age crooners, of which Columbo was an undisputed giant. He was a skilful exponent of a radio-friendly conversational singing style, that not only exuded sex appeal but addressed the listener in a one-on-one personal way. The crooner was pop's first big adventure!

John Lennon said of Elvis: 'Nothing affected me until I heard Elvis. Without Elvis, there would be no Beatles'. And you could equally say, without Crosby and Columbo, there would be no Sinatra and Cole, hence no Krall and Connick Jr. The crooner (he of the Set Voice) is a thing of the long gone past and forever will be. The crooning sound though will always have a part to play on the pop world stage. There'll always be a talented enough singer who will take up the challenge of the crooner template

ESSAY

and bend it to their will; succeeding at saying something refreshingly new.

Time would reveal it was the Set Voice that fell out of fashion and faded into obscurity, not the actual crooning sound itself, which would stand the test of time. But if you wish to go down the genuine crooner pathway, then you must wake up the archaic Set Voice from its deep state of sleep. Brook Benton did just that in the 60s and magnificently got away with! But sixty years later—in a 21st century whose ears have become so attuned to a Raw vocal sound—resurrecting the Set Voice and making it sell, is a tall singing order indeed.

It's easy therefore to dismiss Russ Columbo as a singing museum piece, as a non-relevant vocalist from a bygone era. After all, singers just don't sound like that anymore, do they? But there is a piece of the golden age crooner in every soul that stands in front of or holds a microphone. The sound of the golden age crooner is the sound of your vocal roots, no matter what style of music you sing in. And you can hear traces of the crooner in most genres of popular music, of which reggae and country are chief examples.

We have gone on quite a journey, and I hope the crooning sound will no longer be 'hard to describe' now you have read this essay. I also hope that my writing has made you see the epitaph *crooner* in a fresh light. What I have learned most of all, from my examination of the golden age crooners, is that the human singing voice is multi-dimensional; having a wealth of technical possibilities at its disposal. If you are serious about your vocal art, it would serve you well to explore your microphoned singing past from its earliest beginnings. You might just discover something valuable along the way; something that will leave you artistically better off!

Oh, and one last thing. And I address this to you, dear Google. Perhaps a more fitting and accurate representation of the epitaph *crooner* would be thus.

A singer, typically a male one, who sings sentimental songs in a soft, low **set** voice.

Sebastian Martin Selby

AFTERWORD ... The life so short; the craft so long to learn — Hippocrates

Singing is ultimately a form of emotional release. The person who uses their voice as an amplifying medium to convey their emotions, is a person who is keeping alive one of the most sensuous forms of human expression ever realised—the act of creating music through your voice.

The history of pop will forever be an eventful one, but a simple tradition firmly stands: a voice and a microphone joining hands to create meaningful art. It's the musical love affair between these two entities that has been the soundtrack to our lives for close to a hundred years, and that continues to vitalise our culture.

Ask yourself the critical question. What is my singing goal? Did you read this manual to help improve the way you sing happy birthday to a loved one come the special day? Or to up your performances of the songs you like to sing at your local pub or bar on Karaoke night? Or do you have bigger ambitions to be on the world stage, standing under the spotlight performing in front of thousands? If your aim is to headline arenas, then you have to take your craft dead serious. To possess an exceptional singing voice is the ultimate musical prize. Commit to your art at all costs and never stop believing.

I have set the stage and now it is up to you to play your vocal part. I have shown you the correct singing pathway; venture down it, and you will find the voice you are looking for. Good luck, and remember, there is always a place in this world for someone who can sing, and sing well!

Sebastian Martin Selby

GLOSSARY OF ORIGINAL VOCAL TRAINING TERMINOLOGY

Lesson 1: Solid Singing Foundation, Quality of Sound, United Vocal Front: **P6**
Vocal Breakdown, Vocal Cord Exertion: **P8**
Sound Expectation: **P9**
Precision Communication, Scale Effect: **P10**
Vocal Start-Up, Air-Extended: **P11**
Breathy Note Mentality: **P14**
Discreet Air Consumption: **P15**
Covert Technique: **P16**
Juxtaposition Mentality, Vocal Juxtaposition: **P17**
Levelled Singing, The Secret Technique: **P18**
Air Status: **P20**

Lesson 2: Centre Action, correct middle tone, Vocal Centralisation: **P27**
Vocal Maximisation, Vocal Ease Zone, Ease of Sound: **P28**
Vocal Merge: **P29**

Lesson 3: Vocal Contrast: **P33**
Purity of Sound: **P34**
Separation of Sound, Say-Singing: **P35**
Vocal Thinking Action, Vocal line similitude
Vocal Character Consistency: **P36**

Lesson 4: Slow the whole thing down, Singing at Ease: **P38**

Lesson 5: Singing Out, Fearless Vocal Mode: **P41**
Vocal Weight Distribution: **P42**

Lesson 6: Stomach Mindset: **P43**
From The Stomach Assurance, Stomach Activation: **P45**
Sounding Out: **P46**

Lesson 7: Throat Disengagement, Throat Conscious: **P48**
Note Gliding, Vocal Containment: **P50**

GLOSSARY OF ORIGINAL VOCAL TRAINING TERMINOLOGY

Lesson 8: Sky Note, Sky Zone: **P52**
    Bottom Note, Bottom Zone: **P55**
    Low Note Persona Mode: **P56**

Lesson 9: Impact Voice: **P59**

Lesson 10: Modern Vocalism, Open-Minded Singer, Sound-Play,
    Rhythm-Play, Phrasing Cooperative: **P62**
    Dynamic Line Approach, Lyric Sculpture,
    Vocal Highlighting: **P63**
    Active Pausing, Present Your Vocal Lines in Stages: **P64**

Lesson 11: The Seeking Mind Frame, Familiarity Disposition,
    The Alternative: **P68**
    Detailed Vocal Expressiveness: **P69**

Lesson 12: Counting on the divine, Vocal Mosaic: **P70**
    Reception Mode: **P72**

Lesson 13: Vocal Stronghold, SPDS, Cast-Iron Throat: **P74**
    Freedom Singing Session: **P75**

Lesson 14: Recognisable Factor, Commercial Vocal Trap
    Reference Voice: **P78**

Lesson 15: Positive Recording Outlook, Vocal shield: **P80**
    Levelled Singing Environment, Central Vocal Perspective
    Voice Preservation Recording Mode: **P81**
    One-Inch Singing Discipline, Central Discipline: **P82**
    Singer at ease Environment: **P83**
    Fear No Note Mindset: **P85**

Lesson 16: Vocal Intensity: **P89**

Printed in Great Britain
by Amazon